THE HUMAN BODY

A Firefly Book

Published by Firefly Books Ltd. 2006

First printing

Published in the United States by
Firefly Books (U.S.) Inc.
P.O. Box 1338, Ellicott Station
Buffalo, New York 14205

Published in Canada by
Firefly Books Ltd.
66 Leek Crescent
Richmond Hill, Ontario L4B 1H1

Created and produced in Italy by
McRae Books
Borgo Santa Croce
8 – 50122, Florence

SERIES EDITOR: Anne McRae
ILLUSTRATORS: Studio Stalio (Alessandro Cantucci, Fabiano Fabbrucci and Andrea Morandi), Studio Inklink, Alessandro Bartolozzi, Manuela Cappon, Sauro Giampaia, Paula Holguín, Paola Ravaglia and Ivan Stalio
ART DIRECTOR: Marco Nardi
EDITORS: Claire Moore and Vicky Egan
PICTURE RESEARCHER: Chris Hawkes
Repro: Litocolor, Florence
PHOTOS: pp. 48–49 © Corbis Conrasto

Publisher Cataloging-in-Publication Data (U.S.)

Hawkes, Chris.
  The human body : uncovering science / Chris Hawkes.
[52] p. : col. ill. ; cm.
Includes index.
Summary: Illustrated guide to the human body, covering anatomy and genetics.
ISBN 1-55407-135-6
1. Human anatomy -- Juvenile literature. 2. Body, Human -- Juvenile literature. 3. Human physiology -- Juvenile literature. I. Title.
611 dc22   QM27.H39 2005

Library and Archives Canada Cataloguing in Publication

Hawkes, Chris
  The human body : uncovering science / Chris Hawkes.
Includes index.
ISBN 1-55407-135-6
1. Body, Human–Juvenile literature. 2. Human physiology–Juvenile literature. 3. Human anatomy–Juvenile literature. 4. Human genetics–Juvenile literature. I. Title.
QP37.H385 2006   j612   C2005-904804-2

ISBN 13: 978-1-55407-135-7

Printed in Italy

THE
HUMAN
BODY

UNCOVERING SCIENCE

Chris Hawkes

FIREFLY BOOKS

Table of contents

Pumping Blood, p. 24

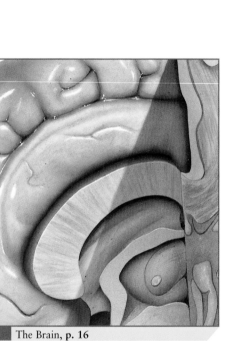

The Brain, p. 16

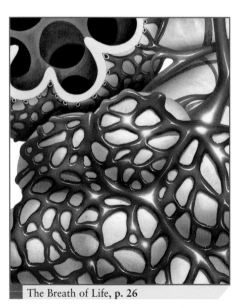

The Breath of Life, p. 26

Introduction

Human beings are extraordinary creatures. Millions of years of evolution have seen the emergence of a race with remarkable capabilities. We can recognize and react to things without even realizing that we are doing so. All the time, hundreds of functions are going on inside our bodies to ensure that we continue to function efficiently.

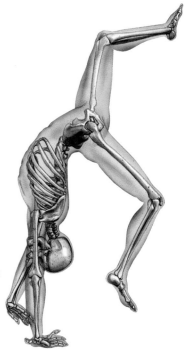

We have an incredible network inside us that carries blood to all parts of the body and, with it, food and oxygen to give us all the energy we need. We can clean our blood, resupply it with all the nutrients it needs and replace old cells. Life-giving blood is pumped around the body by an extraordinary muscle called the heart, which beats up to 100,000 times a day — usually without us even noticing.

We have an extraordinarily complex operating system called the brain, which controls everything we do. It allows us to interpret and respond to everything that goes on around us, and coordinates all the functions that go on inside the body. It has the ability to recognize over 1,000 smells and 10,000 colors. It can remember languages, faces and sounds, and allows us to experience emotion and think with reason.

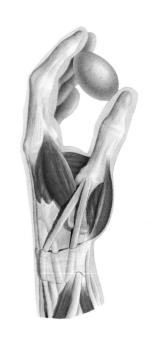

We have the ability to take oxygen from the air around us for use inside our bodies. When we eat, we take all the nutrients we need from food and expel anything that we do not need. We also have the ability to create new life to ensure that the human race continues to survive.

We have an army of cells — the immune system — that fight any hostile invaders from the outside world. The immune system works so efficiently that the only time we know it is there is when something goes wrong and we become ill.

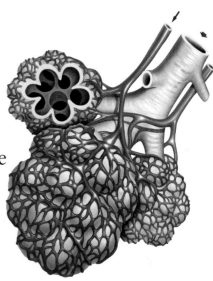

This book will help you to understand what is going on inside your body a little bit better. It covers every aspect of what makes you function properly and will certainly make you realize how special the human body really is.

The Human Body

The human body is an extraordinarily complicated living machine. All its parts — from its solid bones to its liquid blood — are made up of trillions of microscopic cells. Large body parts called organs (such as the heart, liver and lungs) do special jobs within the body and work together to make up different body systems. Together, the body systems perform all the tasks necessary to sustain life. Although we all look different from the outside, everyone — male or female, old or young — shares the same basic body systems.

❶ Muscles
❷ Veins
❸ Tongue
❹ Arteries
❺ Lungs
❻ Liver
❼ Stomach
❽ Colon
❾ Intestines
❿ Bladder
⓫ Trachea
⓬ Aorta
⓭ Heart
⓮ Diaphragm
⓯ Kidneys
⓰ Pancreas
⓱ Duodenum
⓲ Testes
⓳ Skull
⓴ Backbone
㉑ Thyroid gland
㉒ Gallbladder
㉓ Brain

Muscular system

Underneath the surface of the skin, the human body is covered by more than 600 muscles. Triggered by messages sent from the brain, these muscles (often working in what are known as antagonistic pairs) enable us to make all our movements.

Humans are the result of millions of years of evolution. The oldest hominid fossils found so far are over five million years old.

Circulatory system

The heart, blood vessels (arteries and veins) and blood make up the circulatory system. Blood carrying oxygen and nutrients is pumped by the heart through the arteries to all parts of the body. Veins carry the blood back to the heart.

The brain is the most important organ in the human body. If the brain stops working, doctors consider a person to be dead, even if their heart is still beating.

The body is made up of more than 100 trillion cells. Three million of these cells die every minute, but are continually being replaced by new cells.

The reproductive system in male and female bodies works differently, but the other body systems are the same. These systems continually work together to maintain life.

Skeletal system

The skeletal system contains many bones (206 in an adult) that make up the human skeleton. The skull and backbone (the axial skeleton) give us our shape, while the limbs (the appendicular skeleton) act as anchors for the body's muscles and enable us to move. The skeleton also provides a protective cage for the body's major internal organs.

Respiratory system

We breathe using the respiratory system, which uses the nose, throat, trachea and lungs. Air breathed in through the nose rushes down the throat into the trachea and lungs, where oxygen from the air is passed into the bloodstream. When we breathe out, we expel carbon dioxide.

Integumentary system

Made up of skin, hair, nails and sweat glands, this is the body's heat-control system. It allows the body to maintain a steady temperature regardless of outside conditions. When we get too hot, the body produces a salty substance called sweat, which evaporates and helps the body to cool itself.

Reproductive system

The reproductive system functions differently in males and females, with the overall purpose of creating new life.

Nervous system

Consisting of nerves, the spinal cord and the brain, the nervous system processes information from both outside and inside the body and sends messages to the appropriate part of the body. It allows us to react to the outside world and controls what is going on inside our bodies.

Digestive system

The digestive system provides us with energy. When we eat, the stomach absorbs all the essential nutrients from our food that we need to survive and passes them into the bloodstream. Any waste is processed before being passed out of the body.

Other systems

There are other systems in the human body that help ensure our survival. The immune system helps us fight invading viruses or diseases from the outside world. The urinary system keeps the inside of the body clean and removes waste. The endocrine system sends hormones around the body to trigger some activities, such as growth, and to control other activities.

Building Blocks: Cells and Membranes

The cell is the building block of the human body — each one of us is made up of trillions of cells. Each of these cells has a specific function within the body. Cells can also work together to carry out the tasks that keep us alive. Our bones, muscles, nerves, skin and other body tissues are all made up of different types of cells. All cells, regardless of their function, have a similar structure. Around the outside of the cell, holding it together, is the cell membrane. Openings in the membrane allow certain chemicals to pass in and out. Within the membrane is a watery fluid called cytoplasm. This contains specialized structures (organelles) that perform all the different jobs that a cell is required to do. The organelles receive chemical instructions from the cell's control center, the nucleus.

Mitochondria are energy-making centers found in hard-working cells, such as those in the heart muscles or sperm cells.

Cell division

Every human being starts life as a single cell. Through a process called mitosis, this single cell divides to form two new cells. These cells in turn divide, and so on, in a process that continues all the time we are growing (usually until our late teens). After this, cells divide not to permit growth, but to replace cells that have become old or worn out.

Centrioles help to guide chromosomes when the cell divides in two.

Fat store

A layer of fat (adipose) lies just beneath the surface of the skin. The cells in this layer each contain a single drop of oil. As well as providing a vital store of energy and food, fat insulates the body from cold and protects the major organs from damage and injuries.

Ribosomes carry information to and from the nucleus, and help to make new proteins.

The membrane is the cell's outer barrier. It holds the cell together and controls what can pass in and out of the cell.

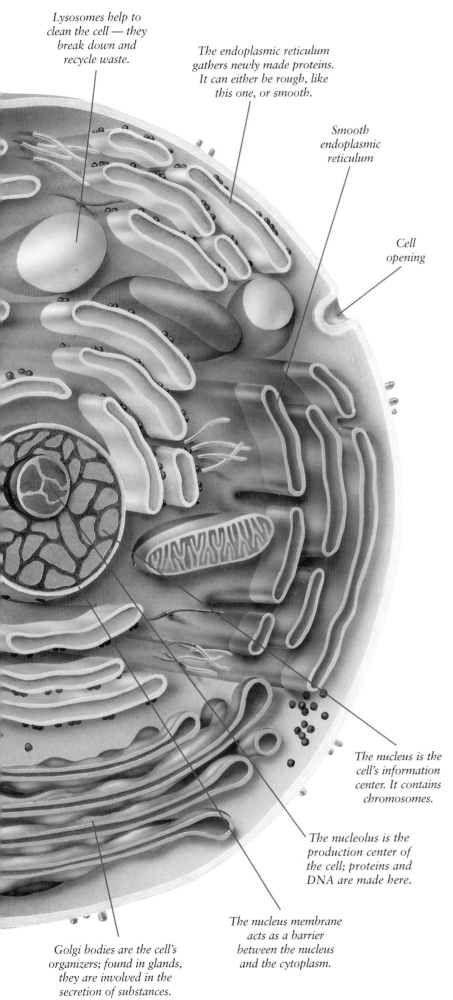

Lysosomes help to clean the cell — they break down and recycle waste.

The endoplasmic reticulum gathers newly made proteins. It can either be rough, like this one, or smooth.

Smooth endoplasmic reticulum

Cell opening

The nucleus is the cell's information center. It contains chromosomes.

The nucleolus is the production center of the cell; proteins and DNA are made here.

The nucleus membrane acts as a barrier between the nucleus and the cytoplasm.

Golgi bodies are the cell's organizers; found in glands, they are involved in the secretion of substances.

Tissue cells

Collections of particular kinds of cells group together to form substances called tissues — for example, muscle tissue or nerve tissue. A fluid called "tissue fluid" fills the spaces between the tissue cells. "Connective tissue" forms between the different types of tissue, and comes in many forms, such as flexible cartilage, hard bone and liquid blood.

DIFFERENT TYPES OF CELLS

Cells come in different shapes and sizes depending on the task they have to perform inside the body.

1 Nerve cells: these are very long with star-shaped heads. They carry signals throughout the body, making contact with other cells.

2 Muscle cells: these consist of long lines of fibers that contract to help the muscle move.

3 Skin cells: these are flat cells that fit into each other like pieces of a jigsaw puzzle to form the body's outer barrier.

4 Blood cells: these can be either red or white. They are carried in the bloodstream and help to provide the body with nutrients and fight infection.

5 Sperm cells: made by males, these are tadpole-shaped cells that, when released inside a female, swim toward her egg cell. They carry the male's chromosomes.

6 Egg cell: found in females, they are round and carry the female's chromosomes. A conception occures when an egg cell is fertilized by a man's sperm.

7 Intestine cells: these have a frilly surface; one of their functions is to help us absorb nutrients from food.

The Bare Bones

Forearm bone (radius)

Forearm bone (ulna)

The skeleton is a mobile framework of hard bones (206 in an adult), flexible cartilage and tough ligaments. Holding the body together, it provides a protective cage for the body's vital organs. The skull, for example, protects the brain; and in the chest, 12 pairs of ribs curve from the spine to the front of the chest to protect the heart, lungs and liver. The ribs are linked to the breastbone (sternum) by flexible cartilage. Anchored to the skeleton are the body's muscles. The skeleton has two main parts: the "axial" skeleton, made up of the skull and spine; and the "appendicular" skeleton — the arms, shoulders, legs and hipbone (pelvis). The places where bones meet are called joints.

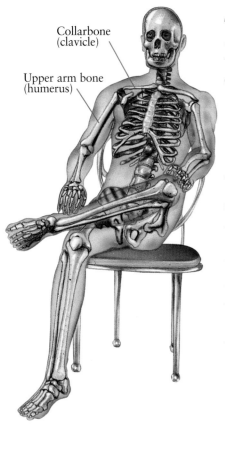

Collarbone (clavicle)

Upper arm bone (humerus)

Thighbone (femur)

The largest bone in the human body is the thighbone (femur), which is about 20 inches (50 cm) long in a man. The smallest bone, at about 1/5 inch (5 mm) long, is the stirrup (stapes) bone, found deep inside the ear.

The largest joint in the body is the knee (right). As in other joints, ligaments hold the bones together and stop them from slipping sideways. A rubbery tissue called cartilage prevents the bones from rubbing against each other and acts as a shock absorber during exercise.

There are several different types of vertebrae in the spine. Seven cervical vertebrae support the head and neck; 12 thoracic vertebrae hold the ribs in place; five lumbar vertebrae support the weight of the back; five fused vertebrae make up the sacrum (located between the two hipbones); and four fused vertebrae at the base of the spine form the coccyx (which in some animals forms the tail).

Ligaments and cartilage

Ligaments, made of a tough, fibrous tissue, are anchored to the ends of the bones in a joint, holding them together and providing stability. Sometimes a joint can become dislocated and the ligaments torn. A person whose ligaments are looser than normal is said to be "double jointed." Cartilage pads the ends of the bones, allowing them to slide past each other without wearing down. It is also found in the flexible part of the nose, the outer ear and the backbone.

Shinbone (tibia)

Calf bone (fibula)

The skull of a newborn baby has tiny gaps, called fontanelles, between the bones. These allow the bones of the skull to move together slightly as the baby is pushed through the mother's birth canal. The skull expands as the baby starts to grow, and by 18 months the fontanelles have been replaced by bone.

Bones

Most people imagine bone to be dry and lifeless. But in fact about a quarter of it is water, it is packed with blood vessels and nerves, and it has the ability to repair itself if it is broken. Bone tissue (matrix) contains two main ingredients: mineral salts, which help to give bones their strength, and a protein called collagen, which gives them flexibility.

Below: The mobility of hand joints allows a flamenco dancer to make a rapid succession of complex, graceful movements.

Middle phalanx bone

Distal phalanx bone

Proximal phalanx bone

Metacarpal bone

Skull and spine

Twenty-one immovable bones and a hingelike mandible (lower jaw) make up the skull — the most complicated bony structure in the body. The skull has two main functions: (1) to support and protect the brain, the eyes and the other sense organs and (2) to form the shape of the face. The spine, made up of 24 separate and differently shaped bones called vertebrae, protects the spinal cord and forms the supporting backbone of the skeleton.

Backbone (made up of separate vertebrae)

Bone's outer layer (periosteum)

Compact bone

Marrow

Spongy bone

Blood vessel

Above: A slice through a bone shows its different layers. The compact outer layer is made of bony cylinders called osteons. Inside is a spongy layer made of tiny honeycomb structures called trabeculae. Spongy bone contains marrow (a jellylike substance). Yellow marrow stores fat and red marrow makes blood cells.

Joints

Without joints — the place where two bones meet — the skeleton would be rigid. Joints allow us to move in different ways. Some joints are fixed (like the skull), some are semimobile (like the spine's vertebrae) and some are mobile (like the knees and elbows).

TYPES OF JOINTS

Most joints move freely and are known as synovial joints. The two main kinds are:

(1) The ball-and-socket joint, found in the hip and shoulder. In this type of joint, the ball-shaped end of one bone fits into the cup-shaped socket of another, allowing the first bone to swivel to and fro and move from side to side.

(2) The hinge joint, found in the knee and elbow. This kind of joint is less flexible, moving only to and fro and not from side to side. It is very strong.

Other kinds of joint include the pivot joint (at the top of the spine) and the saddle joint (at the base of the thumb).

The Outer Layer

Our skin acts as a barrier against the outside world. It protects our internal organs from possible sources of infection and helps control body temperature. It is also an important sensory organ. Skin has three layers. The outer layer (epidermis) is made of tough, interlocking dead cells, which are constantly being worn away and replaced by cells in the lower epidermis. The middle layer (dermis) contains sensors, nerves, blood vessels and sweat glands. The inner (subcutaneous) layer is mostly fat, which helps to keep the body warm. It is also where hair follicles are located.

Body cooler

The body is usually kept at a constant temperature of 98.6°F (37°C). But if we run or do strenuous exercise, our muscles release heat and the body gets hotter. At the first sign of a rise in body temperature, sweat glands in the skin release sweat onto the skin. As the sweat evaporates, it draws heat from the body, allowing it to cool down.

Hair

A person with a full head of hair has over 100,000 hairs on their head. Each day, we lose about 50 to 100 of these hairs. Hair grows from its roots, which are embedded in pits, called follicles, in the skin. As new cells are created in the follicles, long strands of dead cells are pushed out, forming the hair that we see. Oil from sebaceous glands in the skin keeps the hair glossy. Tiny hairs also grow on every part of the body (apart from our palms and the soles of our feet), helping to keep us warm.

Fingerprints

Tiny folds in the skin on each fingertip form whorls, loops and arches. These patterns are called fingerprints. Each person's fingerprints are unique (no one else has the same patterns), so they can be used to identify people. Our footprints and handprints are also unique.

Hair color is determined by the kind of melanin pigment in the follicles. Red melanin produces red hair (top), and dark brown melanin produces brown or blond hair, depending on how much of it a person has.

Below: A cross-section of human skin. Less than 1/10 of an inch (2 mm) thick, it is a remarkably effective barrier against the outside world.

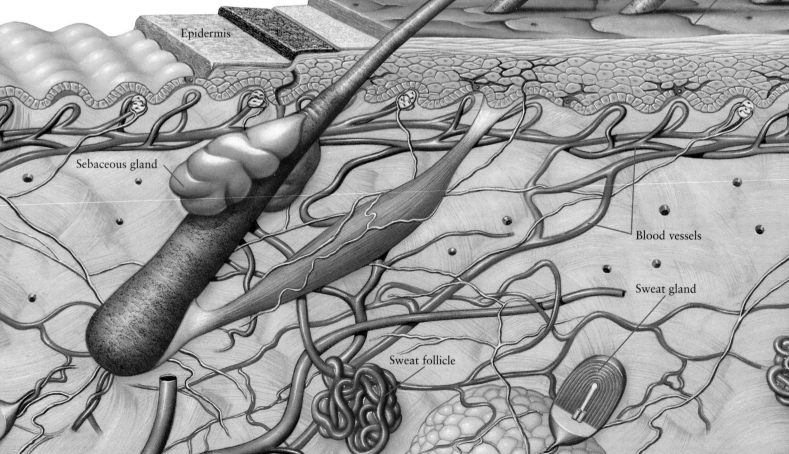

Epidermis

Sweat pore

Sebaceous gland

Blood vessels

Sweat gland

Sweat follicle

Fat

Nails

Nails protect and cover the ends of the phalanges — the thin bones at the ends of the fingers and toes. Living cells produced in the root of the nail divide constantly and push the nail forward, making it grow. Nails typically grow at a rate of about 2½ inches (6 cm) a year. As the new cells push forward, they fill with keratin (the same substance that makes hair) and minerals, making the nail hard. Nails grow faster in summer than they do in winter. The longest human nail ever recorded was 28 inches (70 cm) long!

This microscopic view of a fingernail shows flat cells that are already dead (like hair cells). Fingernails make it easier for us to pick up objects.

Right: A microscopic view of the outer layer of the epidermis. The dead skin cells lock together like pieces of a jigsaw puzzle. They are constantly being shed and replaced.

Shedding skin

The dead cells on the outer layer of the epidermis are constantly being worn away. On average, we lose about 30,000 to 40,000 dead skin cells every minute; but new skin cells are being produced all the time to replace the dead cells.

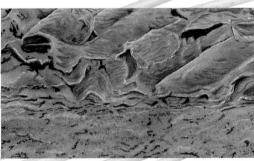

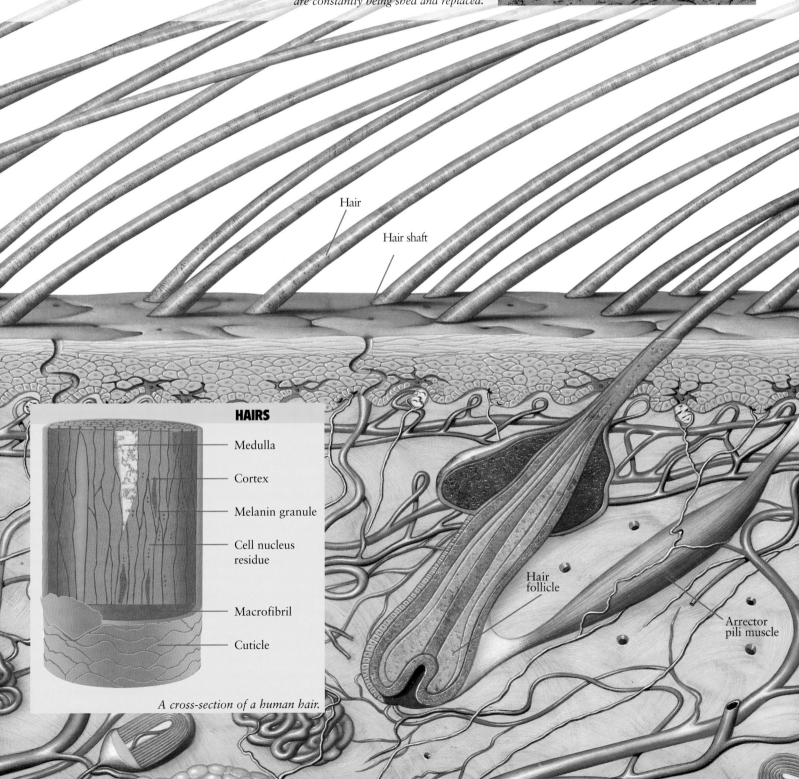

Hair

Hair shaft

HAIRS

Medulla

Cortex

Melanin granule

Cell nucleus residue

Macrofibril

Cuticle

A cross-section of a human hair.

Hair follicle

Arrector pili muscle

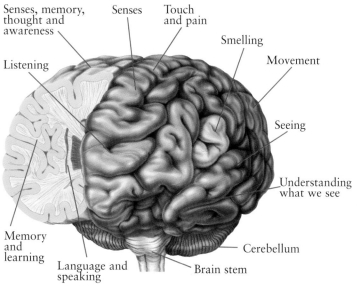

Senses, memory, thought and awareness

Senses

Touch and pain

Smelling

Movement

Listening

Seeing

Understanding what we see

Memory and learning

Cerebellum

Language and speaking

Brain stem

The Brain

The brain is the body's control center. It regulates the speed of our heartbeat and breathing, controls body temperature, processes all of the information we receive from our senses, allows us to move by sending nervous signals to various parts of the body and enables us to think, dream, reason and feel emotions. Although it accounts for only about 2 percent of our body weight, the brain uses about 20 percent of our energy.

Different parts of the brain

The brain is the most complex organ in the human body. It has three distinct parts: the cerebrum, which regulates emotion and conscious action; the cerebellum, which helps us to coordinate our movements; and the brain stem, which controls reflexes, regulates the heartbeat and other functions like digestion, and is the link between the brain and the spinal cord.

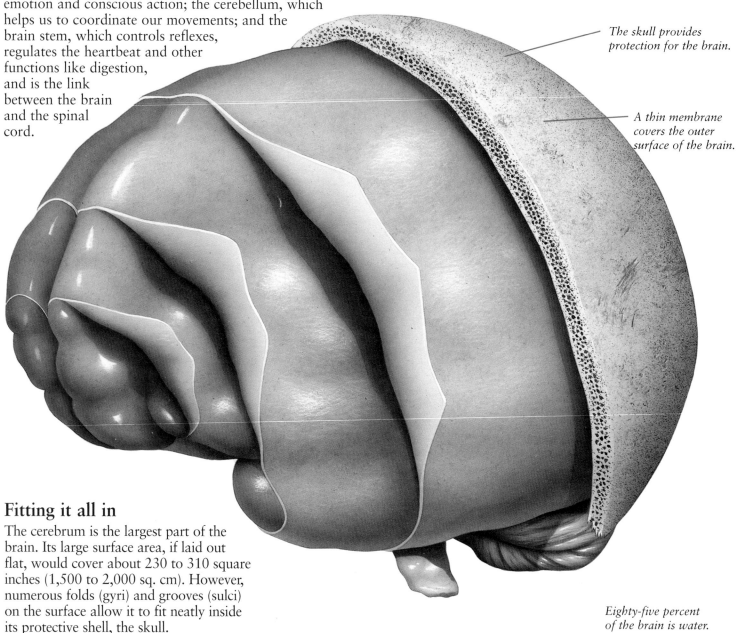

The skull provides protection for the brain.

A thin membrane covers the outer surface of the brain.

Fitting it all in

The cerebrum is the largest part of the brain. Its large surface area, if laid out flat, would cover about 230 to 310 square inches (1,500 to 2,000 sq. cm). However, numerous folds (gyri) and grooves (sulci) on the surface allow it to fit neatly inside its protective shell, the skull.

Eighty-five percent of the brain is water.

Brain waves

Every second, millions of nerve impulses flash along the neurons inside the brain, making patterns of electrical currents called brain waves. These patterns change depending on what a person is doing. If you are awake but resting, alpha waves occur; if you are concentrating, beta waves occur; if you are in a relaxed state (asleep, for example), your brain produces delta waves.

The brain operates on the same amount of energy as a 10-watt light bulb.

The inside of the brain contains a vast network of nerve cells called neurons. A single nerve can send up to 1,000 impulses per second – these are called brain waves.

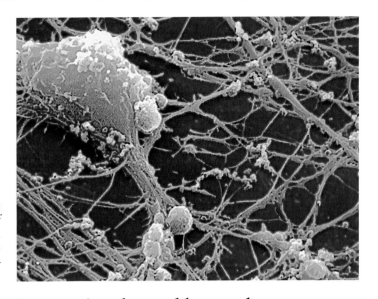

Two sides

The cerebrum (or cerebral cortex) is the large, wrinkled part on the top of the brain. It is divided into two distinct halves, or hemispheres, separated by a groove up the middle. The two parts perform different functions, but are connected and can communicate with each other. When we listen to music, recognize someone or use our imagination, we use the right side of our brains. When we talk, work out a math problem or use logic, we use the left side.

The adult brain has approximately 14 billion nerve cells (neurons) and weighs about 3 pounds (1.4 kg).

Interpreting the world around us

The cerebrum contains all the sensors that help us to receive and interpret information from the outside world. The sensors relating to different tasks are located in different places. Some sensors prompt us to move, some enable us to analyze information and to reason, and yet others relate to emotions, sight, speech and hearing.

The cerebrum is covered with grooves and folds that increase its surface area.

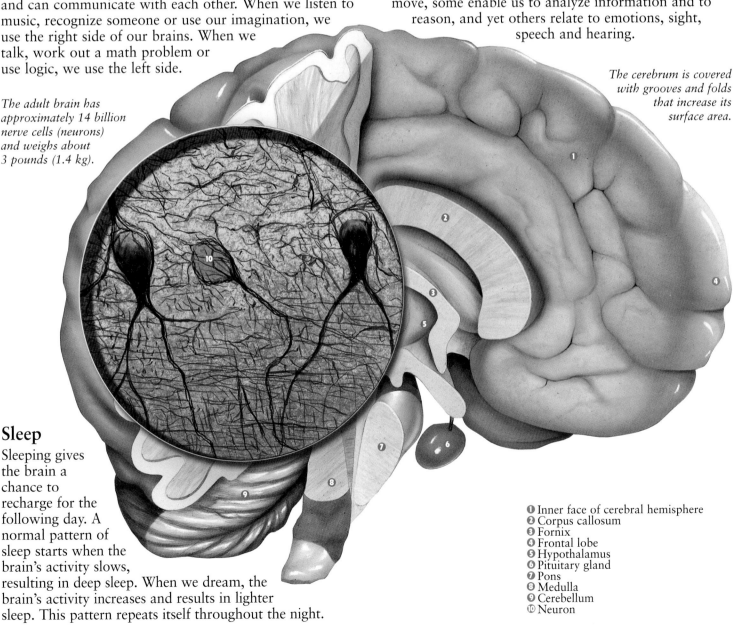

Sleep

Sleeping gives the brain a chance to recharge for the following day. A normal pattern of sleep starts when the brain's activity slows, resulting in deep sleep. When we dream, the brain's activity increases and results in lighter sleep. This pattern repeats itself throughout the night.

❶ Inner face of cerebral hemisphere
❷ Corpus callosum
❸ Fornix
❹ Frontal lobe
❺ Hypothalamus
❻ Pituitary gland
❼ Pons
❽ Medulla
❾ Cerebellum
❿ Neuron

Brain

Spinal cord

The Nervous System

The nervous system is a network of nerves that links the brain to every part of the body. It carries information from sense receptors to the brain, which interprets the information and sends messages back via the nervous system to muscles and organs. The core of the nervous system, the brain and spinal cord, is called the central nervous system (CNS). The network of nerves that spreads out from the spinal cord is the peripheral nervous system (PNS). A third system, the autonomic nervous system (ANS), controls automatic functions such as the heartbeat.

1   **2**

3   **4**

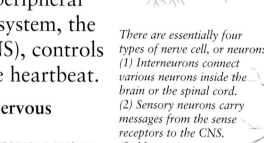

There are essentially four types of nerve cell, or neuron: (1) Interneurons connect various neurons inside the brain or the spinal cord. (2) Sensory neurons carry messages from the sense receptors to the CNS. (3) Motor neurons carry signals from the CNS to muscles. (4) Receptors sense the environment and turn the messages into electrochemical messages, which are then transmitted via sensory neurons to the CNS.

The spinal cord

The spinal cord sits inside the vertebral column, or backbone, for protection, and connects to the brain at the brain stem. Any information received from the body's branching network of nerves is relayed through the spinal cord to the brain, where it is interpreted and the appropriate orders are issued.

Peripheral nervous system

The peripheral nervous system has two main branches of nerves: the 12 cranial nerves in the head and the 31 pairs of nerves that branch off the spinal cord. Numerous other nerves branch off these nerves, winding between the organs and running to the ends of the fingers and toes.

Reflexes

When a doctor gently knocks a hammer against a certain part of your knee, a knee-jerk "reflex action" occurs — you react without thinking. This happens because the spinal cord sends a message via motor neurons to the leg muscle telling it to contract, before the original message has reached the brain.

SPINAL CORD

The spinal cord runs through the center of the vertebrae that together make up the backbone, and is protected by them.

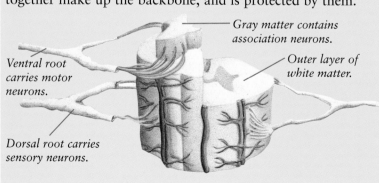

Gray matter contains association neurons.

Outer layer of white matter.

Ventral root carries motor neurons.

Dorsal root carries sensory neurons.

Neurons

Nerves are made up of cells called neurons. Neurons have specialized extensions called dendrites and axons. Axons carry information away from the cell body. There is usually only one per cell, and they can branch a long distance from the cell body. Smooth-surfaced, they can be covered with myelin (a protective sheath that speeds up the transmission of nerve impulses). Rough-surfaced dendrites carry information to the cell body. A cell contains many dendrites, and they only branch near the cell body.

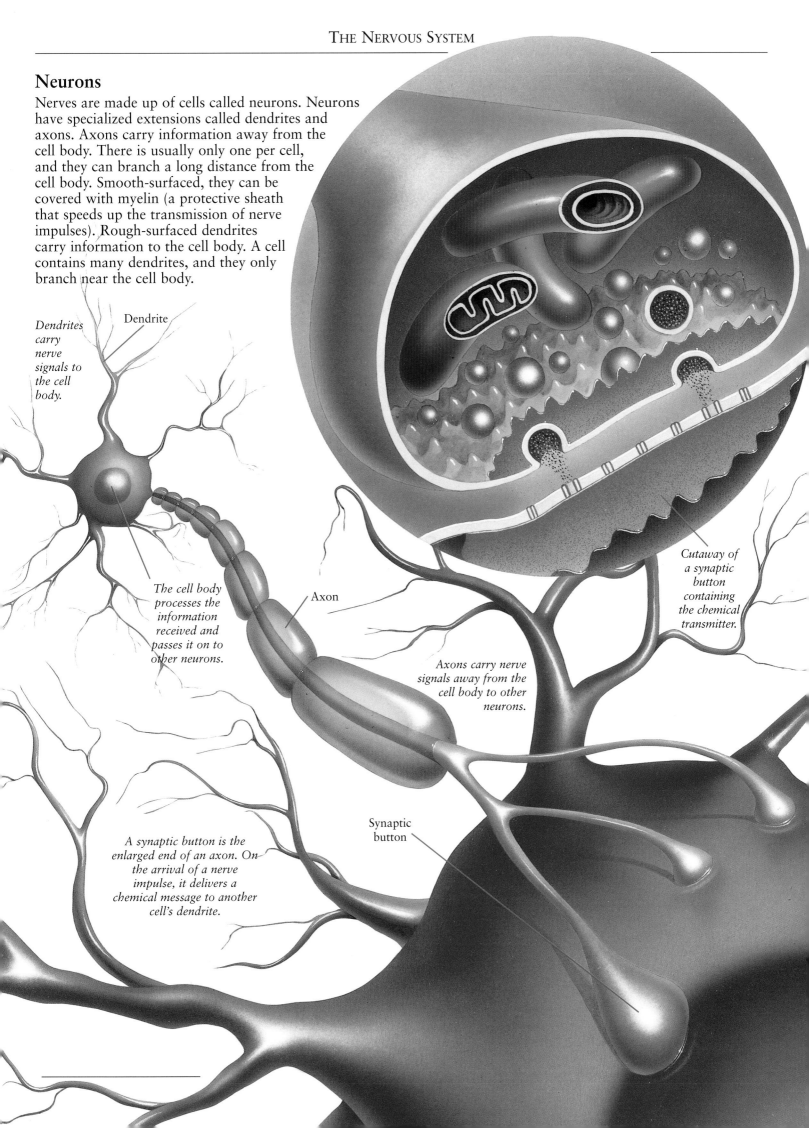

Dendrites carry nerve signals to the cell body.

Dendrite

The cell body processes the information received and passes it on to other neurons.

Axon

Axons carry nerve signals away from the cell body to other neurons.

Cutaway of a synaptic button containing the chemical transmitter.

Synaptic button

A synaptic button is the enlarged end of an axon. On the arrival of a nerve impulse, it delivers a chemical message to another cell's dendrite.

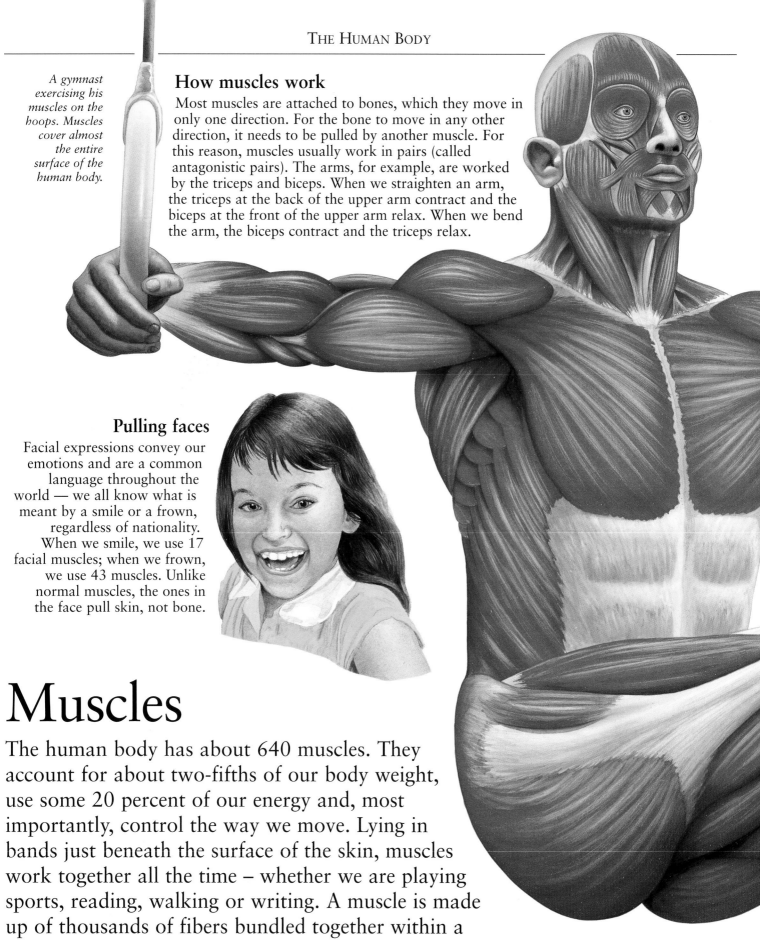

A gymnast exercising his muscles on the hoops. Muscles cover almost the entire surface of the human body.

How muscles work

Most muscles are attached to bones, which they move in only one direction. For the bone to move in any other direction, it needs to be pulled by another muscle. For this reason, muscles usually work in pairs (called antagonistic pairs). The arms, for example, are worked by the triceps and biceps. When we straighten an arm, the triceps at the back of the upper arm contract and the biceps at the front of the upper arm relax. When we bend the arm, the biceps contract and the triceps relax.

Pulling faces

Facial expressions convey our emotions and are a common language throughout the world — we all know what is meant by a smile or a frown, regardless of nationality. When we smile, we use 17 facial muscles; when we frown, we use 43 muscles. Unlike normal muscles, the ones in the face pull skin, not bone.

Muscles

The human body has about 640 muscles. They account for about two-fifths of our body weight, use some 20 percent of our energy and, most importantly, control the way we move. Lying in bands just beneath the surface of the skin, muscles work together all the time – whether we are playing sports, reading, walking or writing. A muscle is made up of thousands of fibers bundled together within a protective sheath, which contains blood vessels and nerves. The fibers themselves can be up to 12 inches (30 cm) long, and are among the longest cells in the body. The more a muscle works, the stronger it becomes, which is why people who regularly work out at a gym have far more defined muscle tone than people who do not exercise.

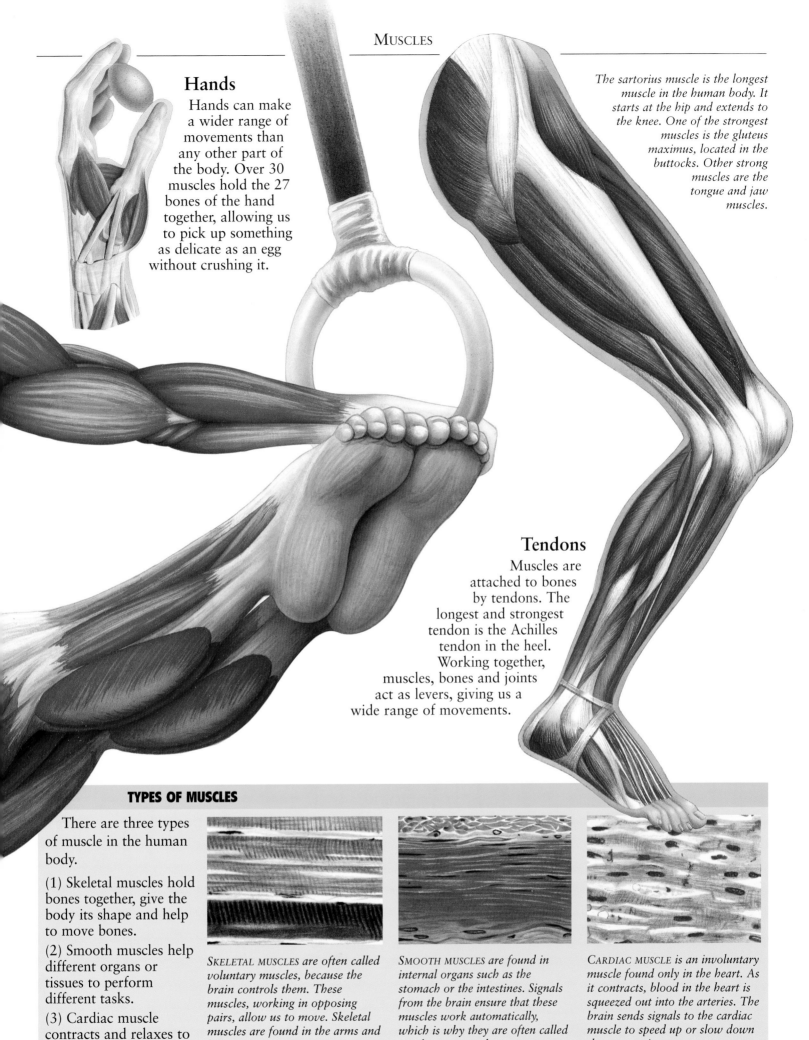

Hands

Hands can make a wider range of movements than any other part of the body. Over 30 muscles hold the 27 bones of the hand together, allowing us to pick up something as delicate as an egg without crushing it.

The sartorius muscle is the longest muscle in the human body. It starts at the hip and extends to the knee. One of the strongest muscles is the gluteus maximus, located in the buttocks. Other strong muscles are the tongue and jaw muscles.

Tendons

Muscles are attached to bones by tendons. The longest and strongest tendon is the Achilles tendon in the heel. Working together, muscles, bones and joints act as levers, giving us a wide range of movements.

TYPES OF MUSCLES

There are three types of muscle in the human body.

(1) Skeletal muscles hold bones together, give the body its shape and help to move bones.

(2) Smooth muscles help different organs or tissues to perform different tasks.

(3) Cardiac muscle contracts and relaxes to make the heart beat.

SKELETAL MUSCLES are often called voluntary muscles, because the brain controls them. These muscles, working in opposing pairs, allow us to move. Skeletal muscles are found in the arms and legs.

SMOOTH MUSCLES are found in internal organs such as the stomach or the intestines. Signals from the brain ensure that these muscles work automatically, which is why they are often called involuntary muscles.

CARDIAC MUSCLE is an involuntary muscle found only in the heart. As it contracts, blood in the heart is squeezed out into the arteries. The brain sends signals to the cardiac muscle to speed up or slow down the contractions.

Pumping Blood

The heart performs the essential role of pumping blood all around the body. Blood not only provides organs and muscles with the nutrients and oxygen they need to survive, but also protects the body from disease. The heart is connected to the rest of the body via an enormous network of blood vessels: arteries (which carry blood away from the heart), veins (which carry blood back to the heart) and tiny, branching capillaries. Laid end-to-end, the body's blood vessels would cover a distance of about 62,000 miles (100,000 km)!

Main veins from body

Main arteries to body

Right atrium

The heart

The heart is the body's built-in pump. Its walls are made of cardiac muscle, which repeatedly relaxes (drawing blood in) and contracts (pushing blood out). Each side of the heart has two linked chambers — an upper atrium and a lower ventricle. Oxygen-poor blood enters the right atrium and is pumped by the right ventricle through the pulmonary artery to the lungs, where it is refreshed with a new supply of oxygen. The now oxygen-rich blood returns to the heart's left atrium via the pulmonary vein before being pumped out to the rest of the body by the left ventricle (the larger of the two ventricles). Valves inside the heart ensure a one-way flow of blood.

The heart has its own pacemaker built into the side of the right atrium wall. Electrical signals make the walls of the heart relax and contract.

Valves in the heart continually open and close to ensure a one-way flow of blood around the body. By placing a stethoscope on a patient's chest, a doctor can listen to the sound of the heartbeat made by these valves opening and closing.

Platelet

Right ventricle

White blood cell

Red blood cell

Blood

Blood flows past every cell in the body, delivering the nutrients and oxygen that the cells need for survival. As it travels, the blood picks up unwanted carbon dioxide, which it carries to the lungs, where it is breathed out. The two main components of blood are plasma and blood cells, made inside our bones. There are three types of blood cells: platelets (1 percent of blood), white blood cells and red blood cells (44 percent of blood). Red blood cells carry oxygen. The average person has about 1.3 gallons (5 L) of blood.

Cardiac muscle needs oxygen to work efficiently. Oxygen is provided by the heart's own blood supply, called the coronary system.

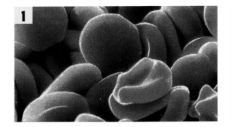

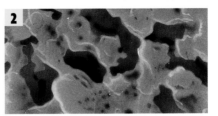

Red blood cells (1) are perfectly adapted for picking up and delivering oxygen. The chemical in the blood that carries the oxygen and exchanges it for carbon dioxide is called hemoglobin. White blood cells (2) act as a mobile army against invading viruses or bacteria. Platelets (3) make blood clot.

Blood vessels

Blood vessels form a vast network that carries blood to every part of the body. This network is made up of arteries, which carry oxygen-rich blood away from the heart (with the exception of the pulmonary artery) and veins, which carry oxygen-poor blood back to the heart. Arteries and veins are linked by tiny blood vessels called capillaries.

Left atrium

Left ventricle

In 1628, people learned for the first time what role the heart actually plays in the body when English anatomist William Harvey published his discoveries about blood circulation in On the Motion of the Heart.

Cardiovascular system

The cardiovascular system is the name given to the heart, the blood vessels and the blood that flows through them. The blood circulates in two stages. The pulmonary system carries blood from the right side of the heart to the lungs, where it picks up oxygen, and takes the oxygen-rich blood back to the heart. The systemic system takes the blood from the left side of the heart and delivers it to the rest of the body.

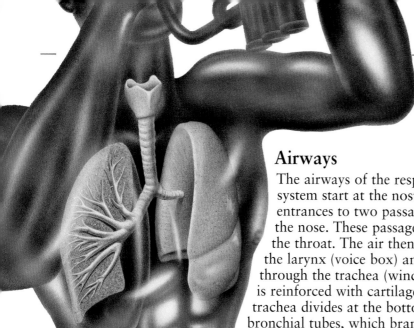

Airways

The airways of the respiratory system start at the nostrils, the entrances to two passages through the nose. These passages join up at the throat. The air then passes into the larynx (voice box) and down through the trachea (windpipe), which is reinforced with cartilage. The trachea divides at the bottom into two bronchial tubes, which branch off into the lungs.

Bronchial tree

The network of airways inside the lungs is often called the bronchial tree. The two main airways (bronchi) branch off to the left and right, dividing into smaller and smaller branches. The smallest of these branches are called bronchioles.

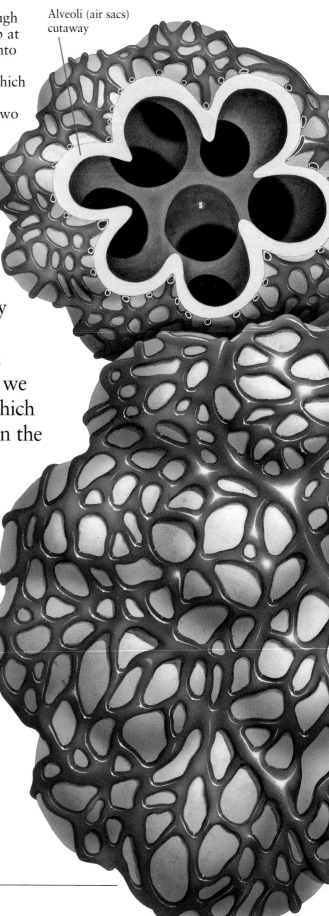

Alveoli (air sacs) cutaway

The Breath of Life

The human body needs a constant supply of oxygen to survive. We obtain it from the air — which is about 21 percent oxygen — by breathing it in using the respiratory system. Air passages carry air to the lungs. There, the oxygen in the air is transferred to the blood. Oxygen-rich blood is then pumped by the heart to the rest of the body. When we breathe out, we expel carbon dioxide, which would be harmful to us if it remained in the body. Exhaled air contains 100 times more carbon dioxide and half as much oxygen as inhaled air.

Take a deep breath

When we breathe in through the nose, air passes into the nasal cavity. Inside the nose, tiny hairs called cilia filter out dust particles. The air is then warmed inside a network of spaces called the sinuses, before it passes into the throat. At the same time that we start to draw in air, our rib muscles contract, pulling our ribs upward and outward, and our diaphragm — a curved sheet of muscle at the base of the chest — becomes flatter. This creates a larger space in the chest, allowing the lungs to expand. When we breathe out, or exhale, the opposite happens – the rib muscles and diaphragm both relax and air is pushed out of the lungs.

A vast network of airways enables us to get all of the oxygen we need into our lungs.

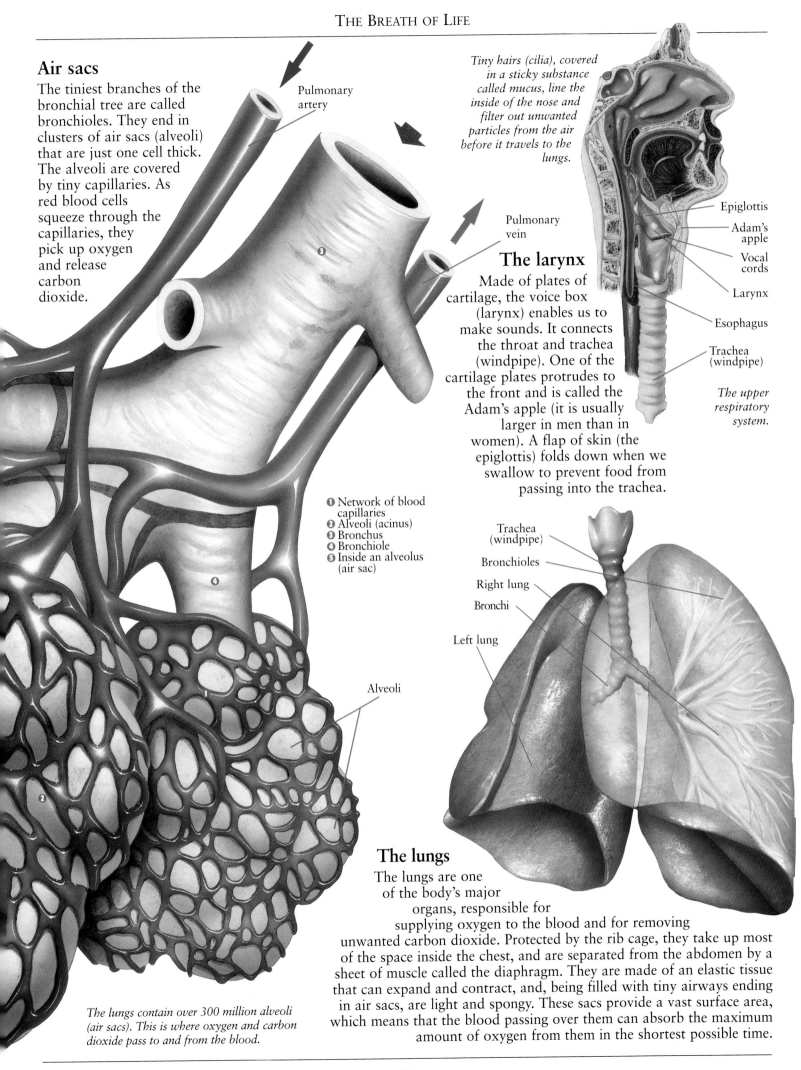

Air sacs

The tiniest branches of the bronchial tree are called bronchioles. They end in clusters of air sacs (alveoli) that are just one cell thick. The alveoli are covered by tiny capillaries. As red blood cells squeeze through the capillaries, they pick up oxygen and release carbon dioxide.

Pulmonary artery

Pulmonary vein

Tiny hairs (cilia), covered in a sticky substance called mucus, line the inside of the nose and filter out unwanted particles from the air before it travels to the lungs.

Epiglottis

Adam's apple

Vocal cords

Larynx

Esophagus

Trachea (windpipe)

The upper respiratory system.

The larynx

Made of plates of cartilage, the voice box (larynx) enables us to make sounds. It connects the throat and trachea (windpipe). One of the cartilage plates protrudes to the front and is called the Adam's apple (it is usually larger in men than in women). A flap of skin (the epiglottis) folds down when we swallow to prevent food from passing into the trachea.

❶ Network of blood capillaries
❷ Alveoli (acinus)
❸ Bronchus
❹ Bronchiole
❺ Inside an alveolus (air sac)

Trachea (windpipe)

Bronchioles

Right lung

Bronchi

Left lung

Alveoli

The lungs

The lungs are one of the body's major organs, responsible for supplying oxygen to the blood and for removing unwanted carbon dioxide. Protected by the rib cage, they take up most of the space inside the chest, and are separated from the abdomen by a sheet of muscle called the diaphragm. They are made of an elastic tissue that can expand and contract, and, being filled with tiny airways ending in air sacs, are light and spongy. These sacs provide a vast surface area, which means that the blood passing over them can absorb the maximum amount of oxygen from them in the shortest possible time.

The lungs contain over 300 million alveoli (air sacs). This is where oxygen and carbon dioxide pass to and from the blood.

Eyes and Ears

Our eyes and ears are the means by which we see and hear the world. The eyes contain about 70 percent of the body's sensors, but although they play a large part in enabling vision, they do not work entirely on their own. The brain also plays an essential role. Sensors in the eyes respond to everything around them and send nerve impulses to the brain. The brain turns these nerve impulses into an image — the thing we see. Hearing also involves the brain. The ears pick up sound waves, which pass through the ear to the cochlea. Cells in the cochlea send signals to the brain, which converts them into sounds.

How we see

Light reflected by an object passes through the eye's cornea and lens, and appears upside down on the retina (an area at the back of the eye). The retina contains millions of light-sensitive cells called rods and cones. Rods give us black-and-white vision and cones enable color vision. These cells send signals down the optic nerve (made of over a million nerve fibers) to the brain, which interprets the image the right way up.

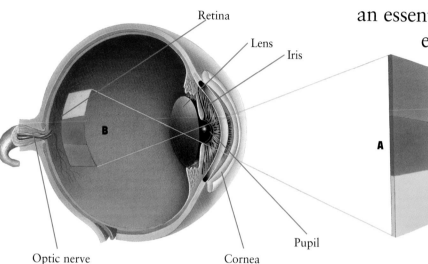

Retina
Lens
Iris
B
A
Optic nerve
Pupil
Cornea

Almost 80 percent of the eyeball is hidden from view, protected inside a cavity in the skull.

Iris and pupil

The colored part of the eye is called the iris, after the Greek goddess of the rainbow. The iris contains a pigment called melanin. Eyes that contain a lot of melanin are brown; those with a little are blue or green. In the center of the iris is a black area called the pupil — the entrance to the interior of the eye. When muscles in the iris contract, they make make the pupil larger, allowing more light to enter the eye. When the muscles relax, the pupil shrinks, allowing in less light.

The eyeball

The part of the eyeball that we can see is called the cornea. It is protected by eyebrows, which prevent sweat from dripping into the eye, and by eyelashes, which keep out dust particles. The eyeball is cleaned by tears each time we blink (about every 10 seconds). Tears contain chemicals that kill any unwanted germs.

The lens

Muscles around the lens help to alter its shape. The lens becomes fatter when focusing light from nearby objects and thinner when focusing light from more distant objects.

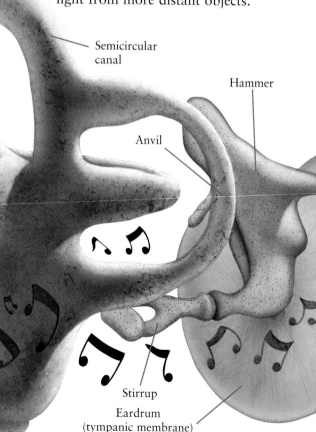

Semicircular canal
Hammer
Anvil
Cochlea
Cochlea (auditory) nerve
Stirrup
Eardrum (tympanic membrane)

The outer, middle and inner ear

The ear has three distinct sections: the outer ear, the middle ear and the inner ear. The earflap (also called the auricle or pinna) of the outer ear is the part we see. It collects sound waves as they travel through the air and funnels them through the auditory canal into the middle ear. Here, the sound waves hit a taut piece of skin, the eardrum, making it vibrate. The vibrations then pass through three tiny bones: the hammer, anvil and stirrup. As the stirrup moves, it vibrates a spiral-shaped, fluid-filled tube called the cochlea, in the inner ear.

Hearing range

The human ear has the ability to detect a huge range of sounds. Pitch — the highness or lowness of a sound — is measured in hertz (Hz), and depends on frequency (the number of sound waves received per minute). As children, we can hear sounds as low as 20 Hz and as high as 20,000 Hz. When we are older, we lose the ability to hear such high-pitched sounds. In comparison, bats can detect frequencies up to 120,000 Hz!

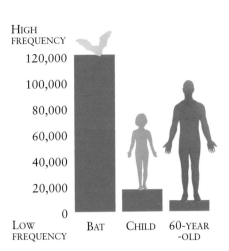

Converting vibrations into sounds

As the vibrations made by the little bones of the middle ear reach the cochlea and knock against it, the fluid inside the cochlea ripples. This sets thousands of tiny hair cells in motion, which trigger messages to be sent via nerves to the brain. The brain converts these signals into sounds.

Balancing act

Tiny hairs in the inner ear allow the brain to know exactly what position the head is in, while hairs inside the semicircular canal send information about its movement. Combining this with other information received from sensors all over the body, the brain is able to send messages to our muscles so that we can change posture and keep our balance.

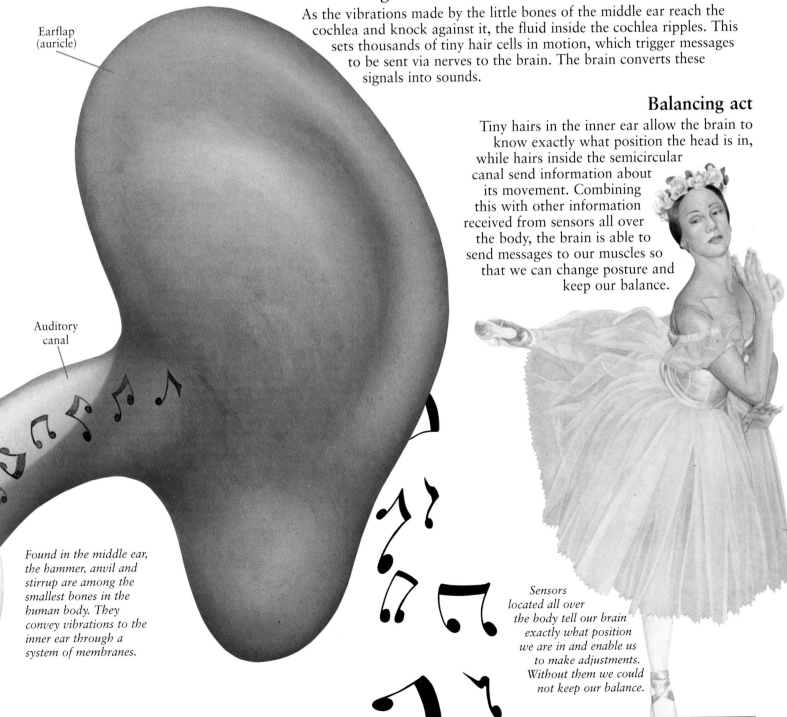

Earflap
(auricle)

Auditory
canal

Found in the middle ear, the hammer, anvil and stirrup are among the smallest bones in the human body. They convey vibrations to the inner ear through a system of membranes.

Sensors located all over the body tell our brain exactly what position we are in and enable us to make adjustments. Without them we could not keep our balance.

Taste, Touch and Smell

Our main senses, in addition to sight and hearing, are taste, smell and touch. Taste receptors send messages to the brain and enable us to detect the difference between thousands of different foods. Smell, which is more dominant than taste, helps us to recognize more than 10,000 different odours. Smell sensors send messages to the same part of the brain that deals with emotions and memory, which is why a smell can sometimes trigger a memory. Touch sensors enable us to recognize temperature and texture.

Papillae

Little bumps (filiform papillae) on the surface of the tongue help us to grip food as we chew it, or lick slippery food, such as ice cream. The tips of these bumps contain keratin (also found in nails and hair), which makes them strong. Bumps that contain taste buds are called fungiform papillae, because they are similar in shape to mushrooms, or fungi. The taste buds are found around the bases of the "mushrooms."

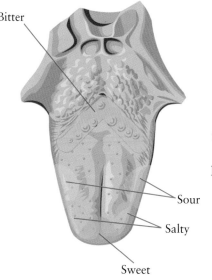

Bitter

Sour

Salty

Sweet

Above: A taste map of the tongue, showing which areas are receptive to particular tastes.

Taste

Our tongue is lined with thousands of taste receptors, which send messages to the brain. The brain interprets the information, allowing us to recognize many tastes. Recognition is a form of protection; the brain tells us, for example, that bitter tastes can be associated with poison, and gives us the opportunity to spit out nasty foods before they do us harm.

Taste buds

The bumps on the tongue contain taste sensors, or taste buds. Each taste bud is made up of about 100 receptor (or taste) cells. The sensation that each cell responds to most determines the overall taste of a particular food. The average person has about 10,000 taste buds, but this number decreases with age. People who smoke also have fewer taste buds.

Below: Through a microscope, the bumps (papillae) on the tongue's surface look a bit like the rough surface of a planet. They help us to grip food as we chew it, and some of them contain taste buds, allowing us to experience the sensation of taste.

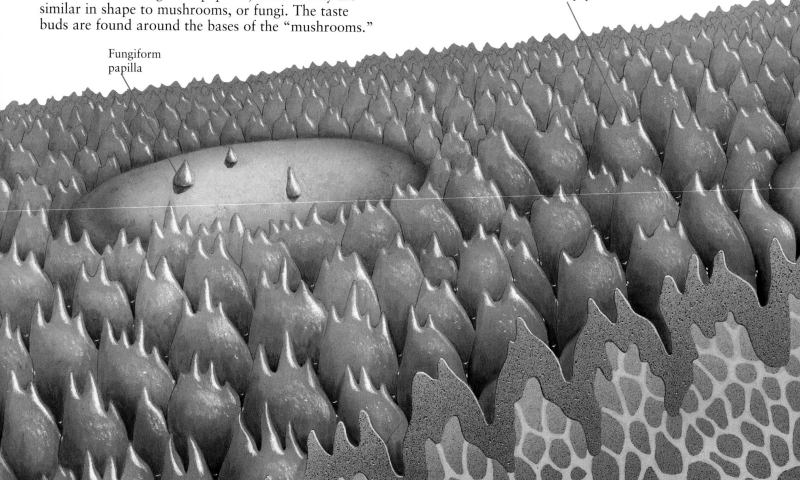

Filiform papilla

Fungiform papilla

Olfactory
membrane

Nasal
cavity

Teeth

Soft
palate

Tongue

Esophagus

The upper portion of the nasal cavity is lined with hairlike, mucus-covered cilia, which capture odor molecules and send messages to the brain.

Nasal receptors

The upper parts of the two sides of the nasal cavity (called the olfactory epithelium) are lined with more than 25 million nasal receptors. Each receptor is a hairlike cilia covered with sticky mucus. When we breathe in odors, their molecules stick to the cilia and trigger messages, which are sent to the brain to be decoded. Sniffing aids our sense of smell because the air we breathe in travels higher up the nose.

Smell and the nose

Smell receptors in the nose send messages to the brain whenever they come into contact with an odor. Our sense of smell is stronger than our sense of taste, which is why food is often harder to taste if our nose is blocked by a cold. Like taste, smell is also a protective sense — our brain associates certain smells with potential dangers.

Sneezing

If you have a cold, or if you inhale dust through your nose, you often sneeze. This reflex action clears irritations fast! A sneeze can expel mucus from the nose at a speed of up to 100 mph (160 km/h).

Sneezing helps to clear irritation from the nose.

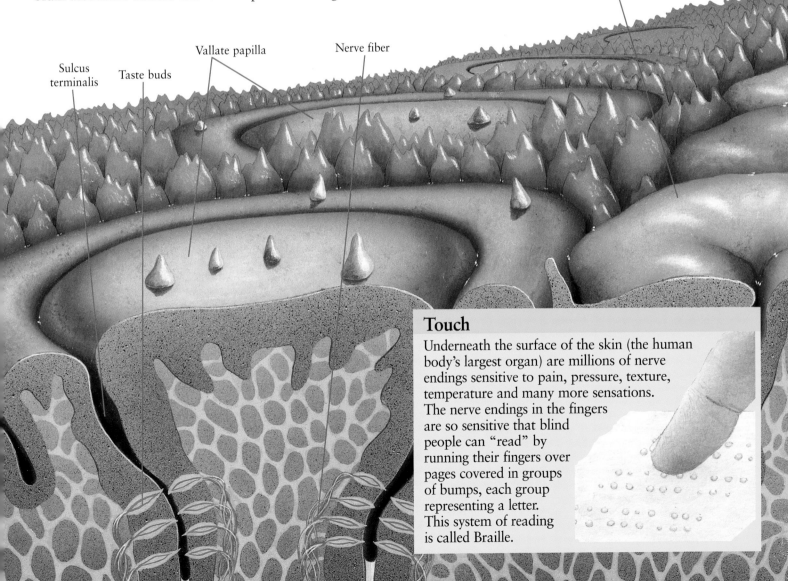

Palatine tonsil

Sulcus
terminalis

Taste buds

Vallate papilla

Nerve fiber

Touch

Underneath the surface of the skin (the human body's largest organ) are millions of nerve endings sensitive to pain, pressure, texture, temperature and many more sensations. The nerve endings in the fingers are so sensitive that blind people can "read" by running their fingers over pages covered in groups of bumps, each group representing a letter. This system of reading is called Braille.

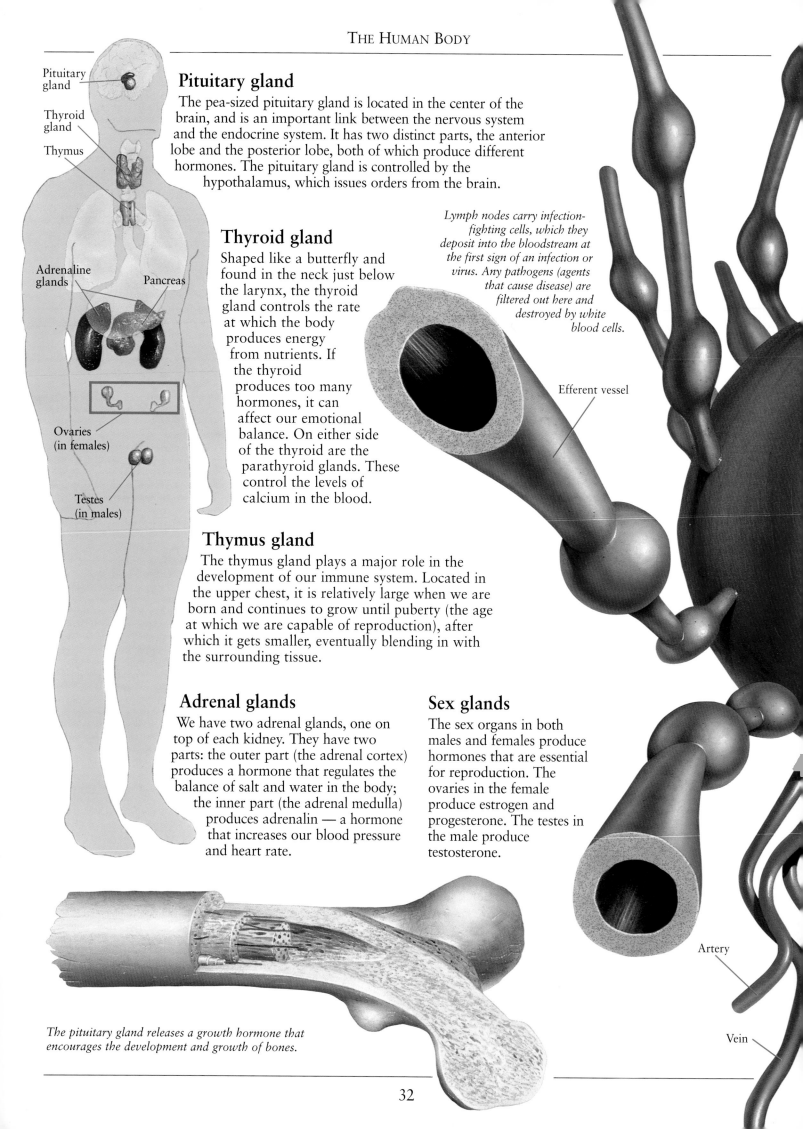

Pituitary gland

The pea-sized pituitary gland is located in the center of the brain, and is an important link between the nervous system and the endocrine system. It has two distinct parts, the anterior lobe and the posterior lobe, both of which produce different hormones. The pituitary gland is controlled by the hypothalamus, which issues orders from the brain.

Thyroid gland

Shaped like a butterfly and found in the neck just below the larynx, the thyroid gland controls the rate at which the body produces energy from nutrients. If the thyroid produces too many hormones, it can affect our emotional balance. On either side of the thyroid are the parathyroid glands. These control the levels of calcium in the blood.

Lymph nodes carry infection-fighting cells, which they deposit into the bloodstream at the first sign of an infection or virus. Any pathogens (agents that cause disease) are filtered out here and destroyed by white blood cells.

Efferent vessel

Thymus gland

The thymus gland plays a major role in the development of our immune system. Located in the upper chest, it is relatively large when we are born and continues to grow until puberty (the age at which we are capable of reproduction), after which it gets smaller, eventually blending in with the surrounding tissue.

Adrenal glands

We have two adrenal glands, one on top of each kidney. They have two parts: the outer part (the adrenal cortex) produces a hormone that regulates the balance of salt and water in the body; the inner part (the adrenal medulla) produces adrenalin — a hormone that increases our blood pressure and heart rate.

Sex glands

The sex organs in both males and females produce hormones that are essential for reproduction. The ovaries in the female produce estrogen and progesterone. The testes in the male produce testosterone.

Artery

Vein

The pituitary gland releases a growth hormone that encourages the development and growth of bones.

Pituitary gland

Thyroid gland

Thymus

Adrenaline glands

Pancreas

Ovaries (in females)

Testes (in males)

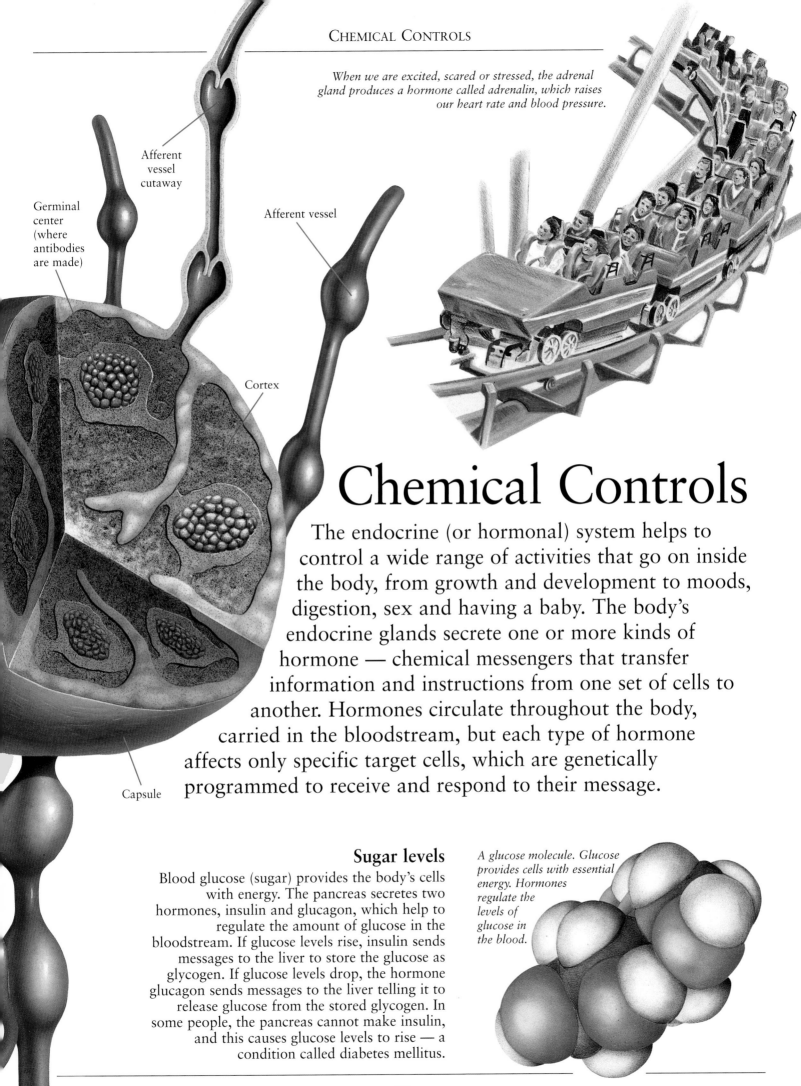

When we are excited, scared or stressed, the adrenal gland produces a hormone called adrenalin, which raises our heart rate and blood pressure.

Afferent vessel cutaway

Germinal center (where antibodies are made)

Afferent vessel

Cortex

Capsule

Chemical Controls

The endocrine (or hormonal) system helps to control a wide range of activities that go on inside the body, from growth and development to moods, digestion, sex and having a baby. The body's endocrine glands secrete one or more kinds of hormone — chemical messengers that transfer information and instructions from one set of cells to another. Hormones circulate throughout the body, carried in the bloodstream, but each type of hormone affects only specific target cells, which are genetically programmed to receive and respond to their message.

Sugar levels

Blood glucose (sugar) provides the body's cells with energy. The pancreas secretes two hormones, insulin and glucagon, which help to regulate the amount of glucose in the bloodstream. If glucose levels rise, insulin sends messages to the liver to store the glucose as glycogen. If glucose levels drop, the hormone glucagon sends messages to the liver telling it to release glucose from the stored glycogen. In some people, the pancreas cannot make insulin, and this causes glucose levels to rise — a condition called diabetes mellitus.

A glucose molecule. Glucose provides cells with essential energy. Hormones regulate the levels of glucose in the blood.

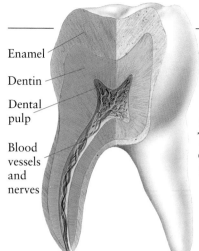

Enamel

Dentin

Dental pulp

Blood vessels and nerves

Teeth

Teeth crunch, bite and generally mash up food in the mouth. Most people have a set of 32 teeth — 16 in the upper jaw and 16 in the lower jaw. Teeth are coated in a substance called enamel, which is the hardest substance in the human body.

During an average lifetime, a person will eat approximately 30 tons of food – the equivalent of 3 pounds (1.4 kg) a day.

Saliva

The first juice that food encounters when it enters the body is saliva in the mouth. Saliva moistens food and makes it slippery, so that it can pass down the throat more easily. It also helps us to digest starchy foods, such as bread and cookies.

Incisors

Premolars

Tongue

Molars

Throat (pharynx), connects mouth to esophagus

Food as Fuel

Food provides us with the raw materials, or nutrients, that we need to make new cells. It is also our fuel, giving us the energy we need to work and play. Without it we would die. Most of the food we eat enters our system in the form of large molecules. The digestive system breaks these down into smaller, simpler molecules, using a variety of special juices, and distributes them via the circulatory system to the rest of the body. Any undigested food is passed out of the body.

❶ Mouth
❷ Teeth
❸ Tongue
❹ Esophagus
❺ Food
❻ Stomach
❼ Gastric juices
❽ Chyme
❾ Stomach lining
❿ Contracting stomach wall

Swallowing

Swallowing — the process of pushing food from the mouth into the esophagus — happens in two stages. First, the tongue pushes chewed food to the back of the throat (pharynx). Then a reflex action pushes the food down into the esophagus.

Uvula

When we swallow, the uvula, which dangles in the middle of the throat, moves upward to prevent food from passing into the nose.

❻

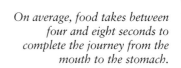

Mouth

Food

The illustration shows the dramatic reaction triggered in the stomach by food. Every mouthful provokes a tornado of gastric juices and a compression of the stomach walls. This breaks the food down into nutrients that will pass into the blood.

Food passes from the mouth down through the esophagus into the stomach, where special juices start to break it down into smaller molecules.

Journey to the stomach

Once in the esophagus, an 11-inch (25 cm) long tube, chewed-up food particles are pushed down toward the stomach by waves of muscular contractions — a process called peristalsis.

On average, food takes between four and eight seconds to complete the journey from the mouth to the stomach.

Stomach

The surface area of the entire digestive system is equivalent to that of a tennis court.

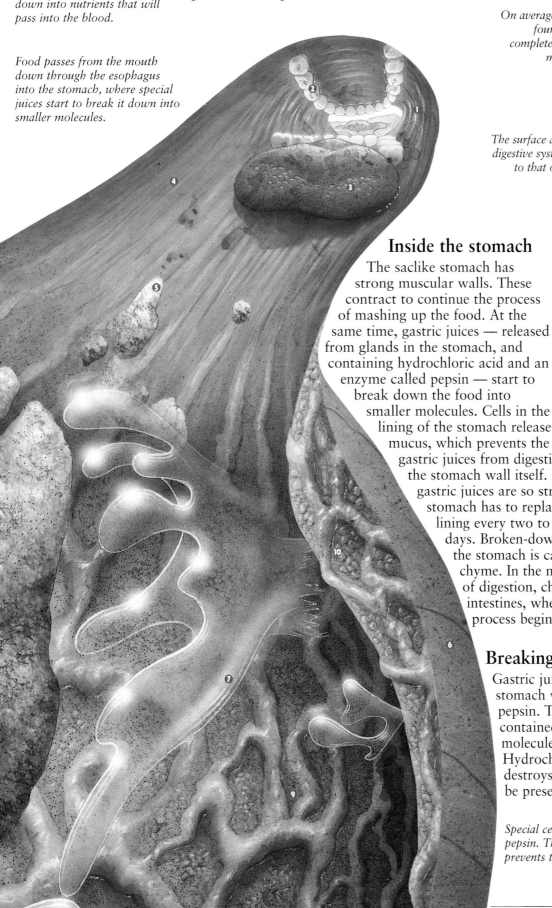

Inside the stomach

The saclike stomach has strong muscular walls. These contract to continue the process of mashing up the food. At the same time, gastric juices — released from glands in the stomach, and containing hydrochloric acid and an enzyme called pepsin — start to break down the food into smaller molecules. Cells in the lining of the stomach release mucus, which prevents the gastric juices from digesting the stomach wall itself. Because gastric juices are so strong, the stomach has to replace its lining every two to three days. Broken-down food in the stomach is called chyme. In the next stage of digestion, chyme passes into the intestines, where the absorption process begins (see pages 38–39).

Breaking it down

Gastric juices released by cells in the stomach wall contain an enzyme called pepsin. This breaks the proteins contained in food into smaller molecules, called peptides. Hydrochloric acid in the gastric juices destroys any harmful bacteria that may be present in the food we eat.

Special cells inside the stomach release pepsin. They also release mucus, which prevents the stomach from digesting itself.

The Intestines and the Liver

After leaving the stomach, broken-down food (chyme) enters the small intestine. Here, the process of absorption begins. Nutrients, which maintain and repair body tissues, are absorbed into the bloodstream and are distributed to the liver and around the body. Useful leftovers (such as water) are absorbed in the large intestine. Waste is then passed out of the body.

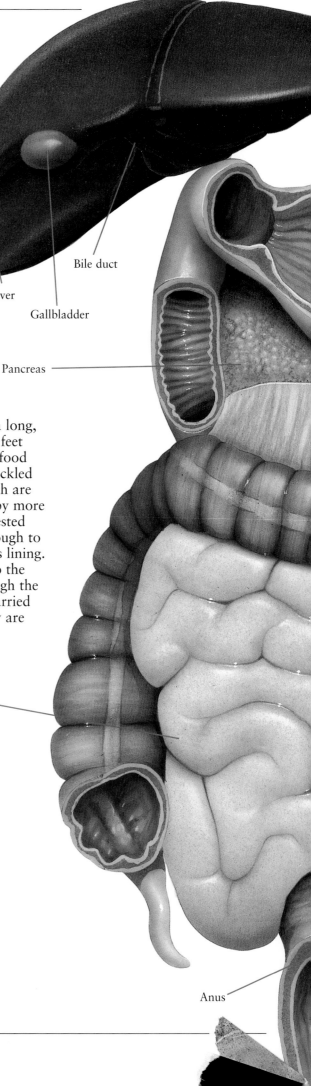

Liver

Bile duct

Gallbladder

Pancreas

Small intestine

Anus

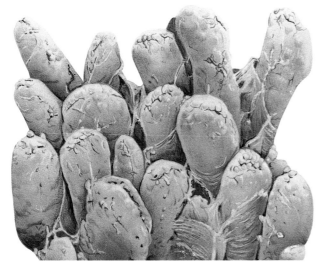

The wall of the small intestine is lined with fingerlike cells called villi. These increase the surface area of the wall to maximize the amount of nutrients that can be absorbed.

Small intestine

The small intestine is a long, narrow tube about 20 feet (6 m) in length. Here, food molecules that have trickled down from the stomach are broken down further by more enzymes, until the digested nutrients are small enough to pass through the tube's lining. The nutrients seep into the blood that flows through the lining, and most are carried to the liver, where they are processed, stored and distributed.

Large intestine

Food molecules that are not absorbed in the small intestine pass into the large intestine, where bacteria kill any potentially harmful substances. Food is not digested in the large intestine, but water is absorbed into the bloodstream. The leftover material, called feces, is passed out of the body through the anus.

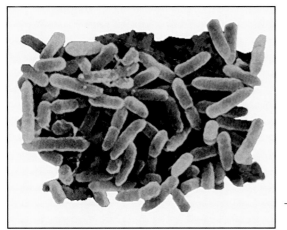

Left: The inside of the large intestine is coated with a 3/4-inch (2 cm) thick layer of bacteria. The bacteria feed on and break down any food remains that were not absorbed in the small intestine.

The liver

The liver — the body's largest internal organ — is a busy chemical factory that performs more than 500 tasks. One of its functions is to process the nutrients in the blood that arrive from the small intestine (about 90 percent of the body's nutrients pass through the liver). At any given time, the liver contains 13 percent of the body's entire blood supply. Once the blood has the right balance of nutrients, it is distributed to the rest of the body. The liver is the only organ in the body that has the ability to regenerate itself — if three-quarters of it is cut away, the remainder can quickly grow back to its original size and continue to function properly.

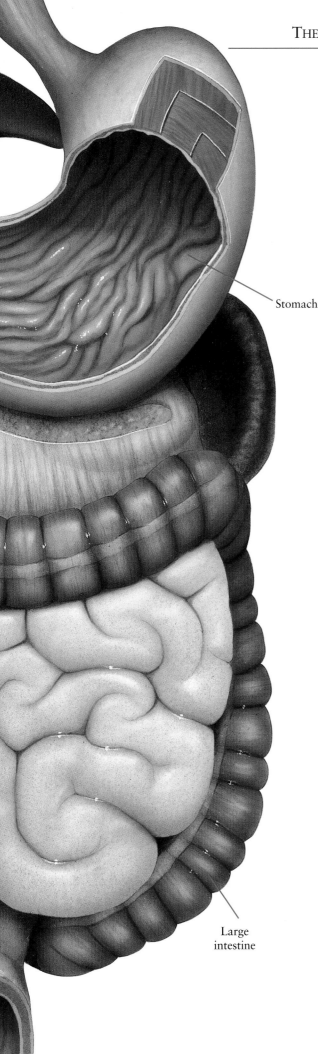

Stomach

Large intestine

Most of the absorption inside the intestines occurs within the first quarter of the small intestine.

Right lobe

Left lobe

Bile duct

Gallbladder

The liver stores sugars and vitamins, and ensures we have enough glucose in the blood.

Inside the liver

Inside the liver, a vast network of blood vessels carries blood to and from the liver cells, which are arranged in patterns around channels (called sinusoids). As blood flows along these channels, the liver cells release substances that process the nutrients in the blood. The newly processed and cleaned blood is then carried away from the liver and distributed to the rest of the body.

Right: Red blood cells passing along sinusoids inside the liver.

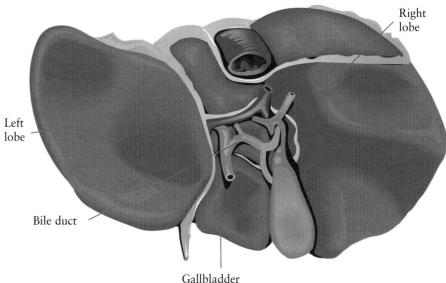

Bile

Bile is a liquid stored in the gallbladder, a muscular bag located next to the liver. Bile is made up of a number of salts that help break down fat into tiny droplets to aid digestion. When we eat, bile is released from the gallbladder through a tube called the bile duct into the duodenum, the first section of the small intestine. The pancreas also makes juices that aid digestion.

Cortex

Medulla

Renal vein

Renal artery

Renal pelvis

Ureter

One quarter of all the blood in the body passes through the kidneys every minute.

Inside a kidney

Blood enters a kidney via the wide renal artery and is dispersed through millions of capillaries in the outer layer, or cortex. Microscopic filtering units (nephrons) in the cortex filter the blood, squeezing out some of the water and toxins. Good substances and much of the water pass back into the blood, but the unwanted water and toxins (urine) flow through the kidney's inner region, the medulla, into a chamber at the center called the renal pelvis. From there the urine trickles out through the ureter to the bladder.

Nephrons

Nephrons are the kidney's filtering units. Each one contains a tight ball of blood capillaries (a glomerulus) and a long, thin, winding tube called a renal tubule. In the glomeruli, water is forced out of the blood by high blood pressure. As the water passes through the renal tubule, any useful substances are absorbed back into the bloodstream and the excess, or waste, forms urine.

The kidneys' job

The kidneys help keep the concentrations of various ions and other important substances within the body constant. They also keep the volume of water in the body constant, and ensure that the acid levels of the blood are kept at a safe level. Any waste acid is removed from the body in the form of urine. The kidneys also help regulate the body's blood pressure, stimulate the production of blood cells and maintain the body's calcium levels.

Sometimes the kidneys cease to work properly. If this happens, a person can be attached to a dialysis machine, which performs the same job as the kidneys — cleaning their blood and controlling their water content.

Descending loop of Henle

Clean blood flows out

40

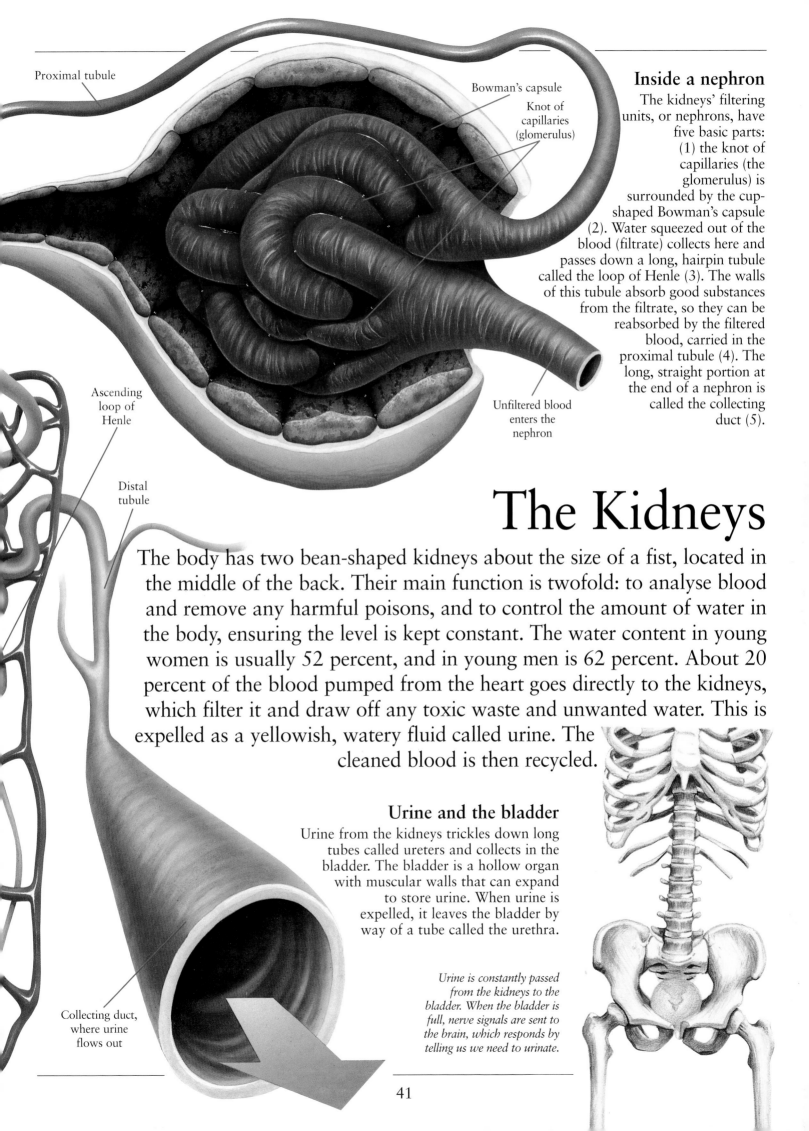

Proximal tubule

Bowman's capsule

Knot of capillaries (glomerulus)

Inside a nephron

The kidneys' filtering units, or nephrons, have five basic parts: (1) the knot of capillaries (the glomerulus) is surrounded by the cup-shaped Bowman's capsule (2). Water squeezed out of the blood (filtrate) collects here and passes down a long, hairpin tubule called the loop of Henle (3). The walls of this tubule absorb good substances from the filtrate, so they can be reabsorbed by the filtered blood, carried in the proximal tubule (4). The long, straight portion at the end of a nephron is called the collecting duct (5).

Ascending loop of Henle

Distal tubule

Unfiltered blood enters the nephron

The Kidneys

The body has two bean-shaped kidneys about the size of a fist, located in the middle of the back. Their main function is twofold: to analyse blood and remove any harmful poisons, and to control the amount of water in the body, ensuring the level is kept constant. The water content in young women is usually 52 percent, and in young men is 62 percent. About 20 percent of the blood pumped from the heart goes directly to the kidneys, which filter it and draw off any toxic waste and unwanted water. This is expelled as a yellowish, watery fluid called urine. The cleaned blood is then recycled.

Urine and the bladder

Urine from the kidneys trickles down long tubes called ureters and collects in the bladder. The bladder is a hollow organ with muscular walls that can expand to store urine. When urine is expelled, it leaves the bladder by way of a tube called the urethra.

Urine is constantly passed from the kidneys to the bladder. When the bladder is full, nerve signals are sent to the brain, which responds by telling us we need to urinate.

Collecting duct, where urine flows out

Reproductive Systems

For the human race to survive, new lives must be produced to replace old ones. The stage at which boys and girls start to produce the special sex cells needed for sexual reproduction is called puberty, and usually happens in the early teens or a little earlier. In males, two testes produce millions of sperm. In females, two ovaries release an egg once a month. When a male's sperm combines with, or fertilizes, a female's egg, conception occurs.

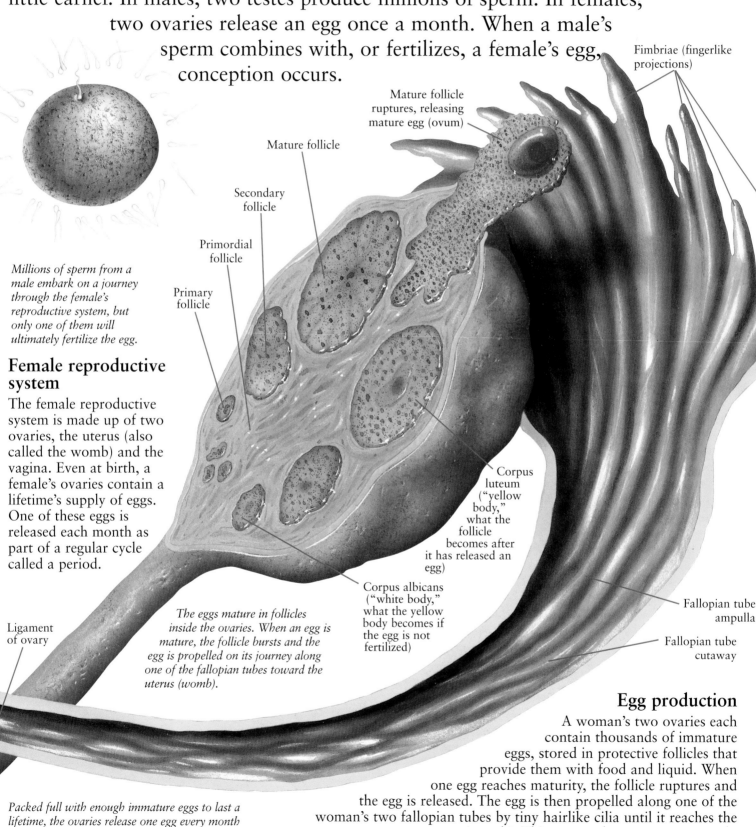

Fimbriae (fingerlike projections)

Mature follicle ruptures, releasing mature egg (ovum)

Mature follicle

Secondary follicle

Primordial follicle

Primary follicle

Millions of sperm from a male embark on a journey through the female's reproductive system, but only one of them will ultimately fertilize the egg.

Female reproductive system

The female reproductive system is made up of two ovaries, the uterus (also called the womb) and the vagina. Even at birth, a female's ovaries contain a lifetime's supply of eggs. One of these eggs is released each month as part of a regular cycle called a period.

Corpus luteum ("yellow body," what the follicle becomes after it has released an egg)

Corpus albicans ("white body," what the yellow body becomes if the egg is not fertilized)

Fallopian tube ampulla

Fallopian tube cutaway

Ligament of ovary

The eggs mature in follicles inside the ovaries. When an egg is mature, the follicle bursts and the egg is propelled on its journey along one of the fallopian tubes toward the uterus (womb).

Egg production

A woman's two ovaries each contain thousands of immature eggs, stored in protective follicles that provide them with food and liquid. When one egg reaches maturity, the follicle ruptures and the egg is released. The egg is then propelled along one of the woman's two fallopian tubes by tiny hairlike cilia until it reaches the uterus (womb). This process happens every month.

Packed full with enough immature eggs to last a lifetime, the ovaries release one egg every month after the female has reached puberty.

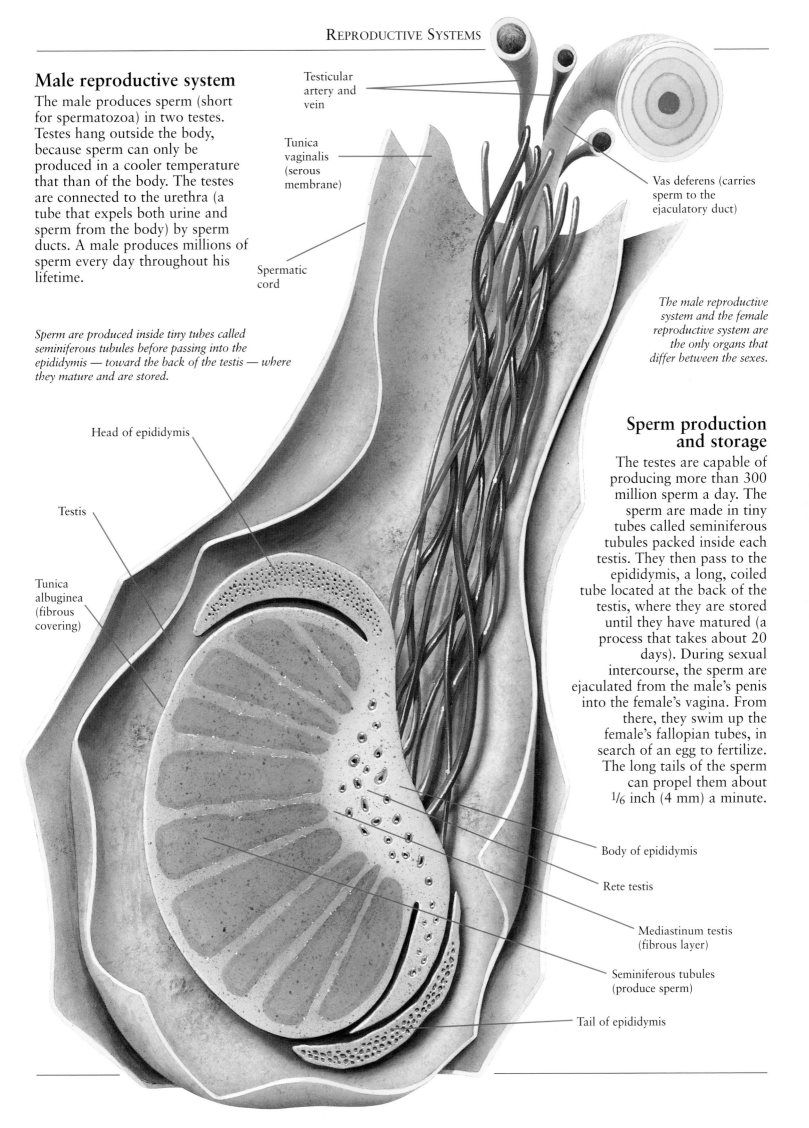

Male reproductive system

The male produces sperm (short for spermatozoa) in two testes. Testes hang outside the body, because sperm can only be produced in a cooler temperature that than of the body. The testes are connected to the urethra (a tube that expels both urine and sperm from the body) by sperm ducts. A male produces millions of sperm every day throughout his lifetime.

Sperm are produced inside tiny tubes called seminiferous tubules before passing into the epididymis — toward the back of the testis — where they mature and are stored.

Testicular artery and vein

Tunica vaginalis (serous membrane)

Spermatic cord

Vas deferens (carries sperm to the ejaculatory duct)

The male reproductive system and the female reproductive system are the only organs that differ between the sexes.

Head of epididymis

Testis

Tunica albuginea (fibrous covering)

Sperm production and storage

The testes are capable of producing more than 300 million sperm a day. The sperm are made in tiny tubes called seminiferous tubules packed inside each testis. They then pass to the epididymis, a long, coiled tube located at the back of the testis, where they are stored until they have matured (a process that takes about 20 days). During sexual intercourse, the sperm are ejaculated from the male's penis into the female's vagina. From there, they swim up the female's fallopian tubes, in search of an egg to fertilize. The long tails of the sperm can propel them about $1/6$ inch (4 mm) a minute.

Body of epididymis

Rete testis

Mediastinum testis (fibrous layer)

Seminiferous tubules (produce sperm)

Tail of epididymis

New Life: Pregnancy and Birth

One of life's vital functions is to reproduce new life — without it, in a century, the human race would no longer exist. Reproduction is the process that sees the reproductive systems of men and women combine, resulting in a fertilized egg. The single egg cell divides repeatedly in the woman's womb until, some 38 weeks later, a baby is ready to enter the world.

A human embryo developing inside its mother's womb. At first it is barely recognizable as a human being, and has a long tail.

After four weeks the embryo already has many recognizable features, such as a head, eyes, arms and legs. The major organs have also started to develop.

A *4 weeks*

B *8 weeks*

Fertilization

As fertilization occurs, the genetic information from the male and female combine to create instructions for a new life. A fertilized egg is called a zygote. The single, fertilized cell immediately divides, and the new cells continue to divide as it moves down the fallopian tube. After about five days it reaches the end of the tube. By now it has become a small cluster of cells called a blastocyst. The blastocyst enters the uterus and sheds the covering it had when it first left the ovary. It then attaches itself to the lining of the uterus (womb). The outer cells will develop into the placenta (the food link between the baby and the mother) and the inner cells will form the embryo.

Early weeks

After four weeks, the process of cell division has created millions of cells that form an embryo. During the course of this repeated cell division, the major organs (such as the liver and lungs) have started to appear. The embryo's heart has even started to beat, and it has begun to pump blood around a small network of blood vessels. There is some evidence of a brain, the beginnings of the nervous system are in place and the limbs have started to form.

After eight weeks

By eight weeks old, the embryo is known as a fetus; it has all the characteristics of a human being. All of its major organs have developed, along with its limbs (including separate fingers and toes). The shape of the face is visible too, with ears, eyes, nose and mouth in place. Within the mother's womb, the fetus floats inside a bag of liquid called amniotic fluid. This helps to protect the baby from any sudden bumps.

Ready for birth

The baby is usually ready for birth after a period of 32 weeks. By this time, it will have developed the senses of sight and hearing, and will be able to move around in the womb. Just before birth, the baby moves to an upside-down position, with its head pointing downward. As pregnancy ends, the muscles of the uterus wall contract to push the baby headfirst through the vagina. As soon as the baby enters the outside world, the umbilical cord (the physical link between the mother and child) is cut.

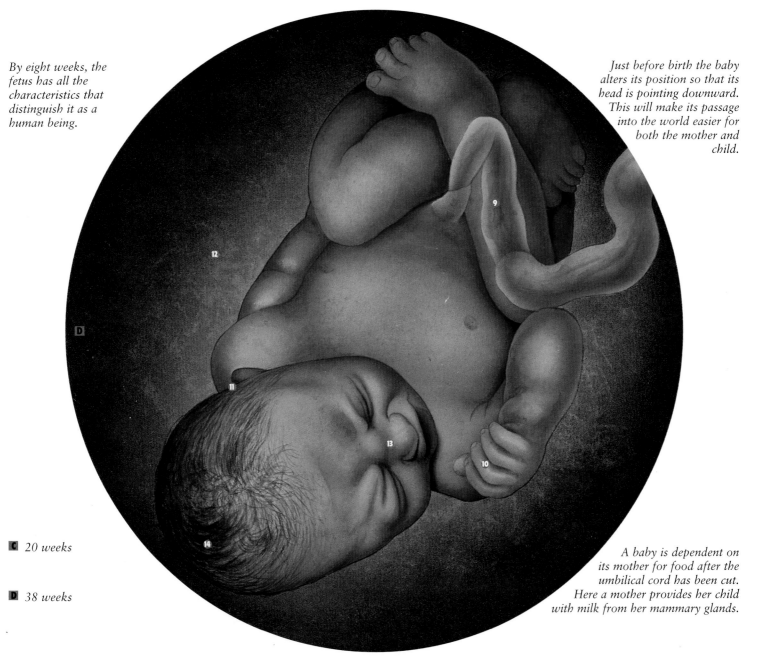

By eight weeks, the fetus has all the characteristics that distinguish it as a human being.

Just before birth the baby alters its position so that its head is pointing downward. This will make its passage into the world easier for both the mother and child.

C *20 weeks*

D *38 weeks*

A baby is dependent on its mother for food after the umbilical cord has been cut. Here a mother provides her child with milk from her mammary glands.

① Muscular wall of uterus
② Head
③ Eye
④ Tail
⑤ Back
⑥ Neck
⑦ Heart
⑧ Arm
⑨ Umbilical cord
⑩ Fingers
⑪ Ear
⑫ Amniotic fluid
⑬ Nose
⑭ Hair

After birth

Once the umbilical cord has been cut, the baby needs a new source of food. This is usually provided by the mother's mammary glands (which have the ability to produce milk). Milk from the mother provides the baby with all the nutrients it needs to grow, and helps to build its immune system.

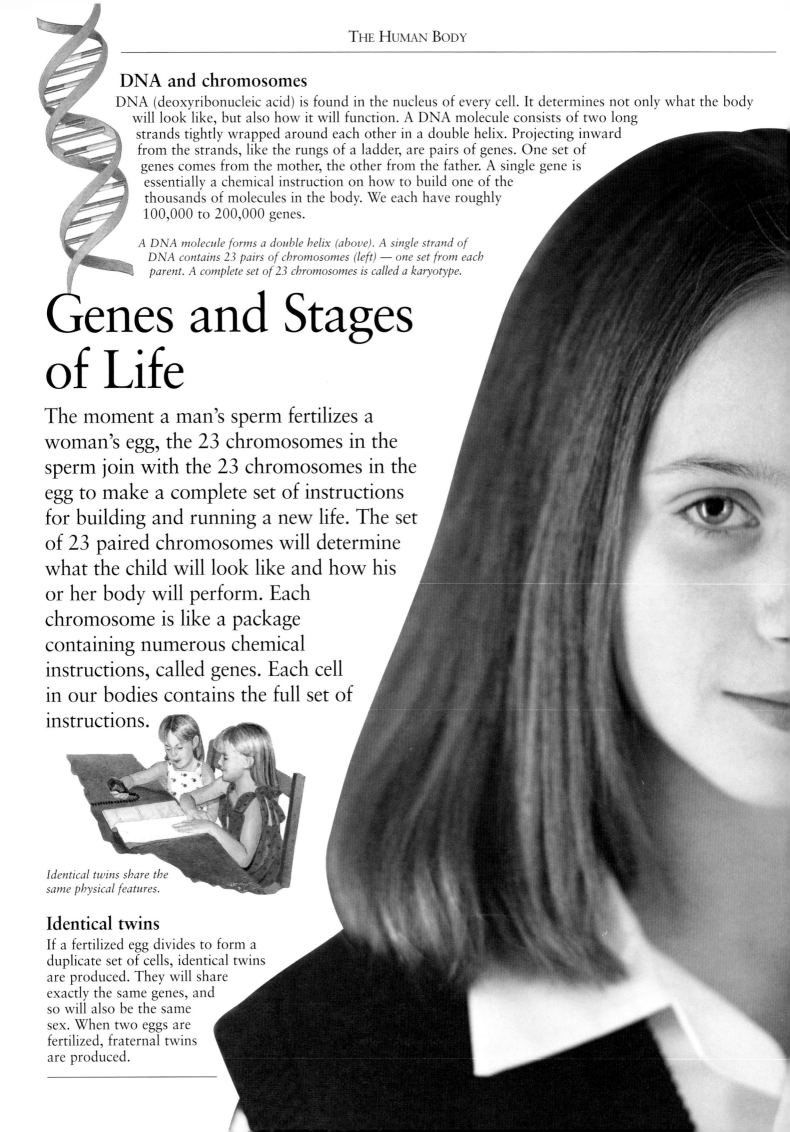

DNA and chromosomes

DNA (deoxyribonucleic acid) is found in the nucleus of every cell. It determines not only what the body will look like, but also how it will function. A DNA molecule consists of two long strands tightly wrapped around each other in a double helix. Projecting inward from the strands, like the rungs of a ladder, are pairs of genes. One set of genes comes from the mother, the other from the father. A single gene is essentially a chemical instruction on how to build one of the thousands of molecules in the body. We each have roughly 100,000 to 200,000 genes.

A DNA molecule forms a double helix (above). A single strand of DNA contains 23 pairs of chromosomes (left) — one set from each parent. A complete set of 23 chromosomes is called a karyotype.

Genes and Stages of Life

The moment a man's sperm fertilizes a woman's egg, the 23 chromosomes in the sperm join with the 23 chromosomes in the egg to make a complete set of instructions for building and running a new life. The set of 23 paired chromosomes will determine what the child will look like and how his or her body will perform. Each chromosome is like a package containing numerous chemical instructions, called genes. Each cell in our bodies contains the full set of instructions.

Identical twins share the same physical features.

Identical twins

If a fertilized egg divides to form a duplicate set of cells, identical twins are produced. They will share exactly the same genes, and so will also be the same sex. When two eggs are fertilized, fraternal twins are produced.

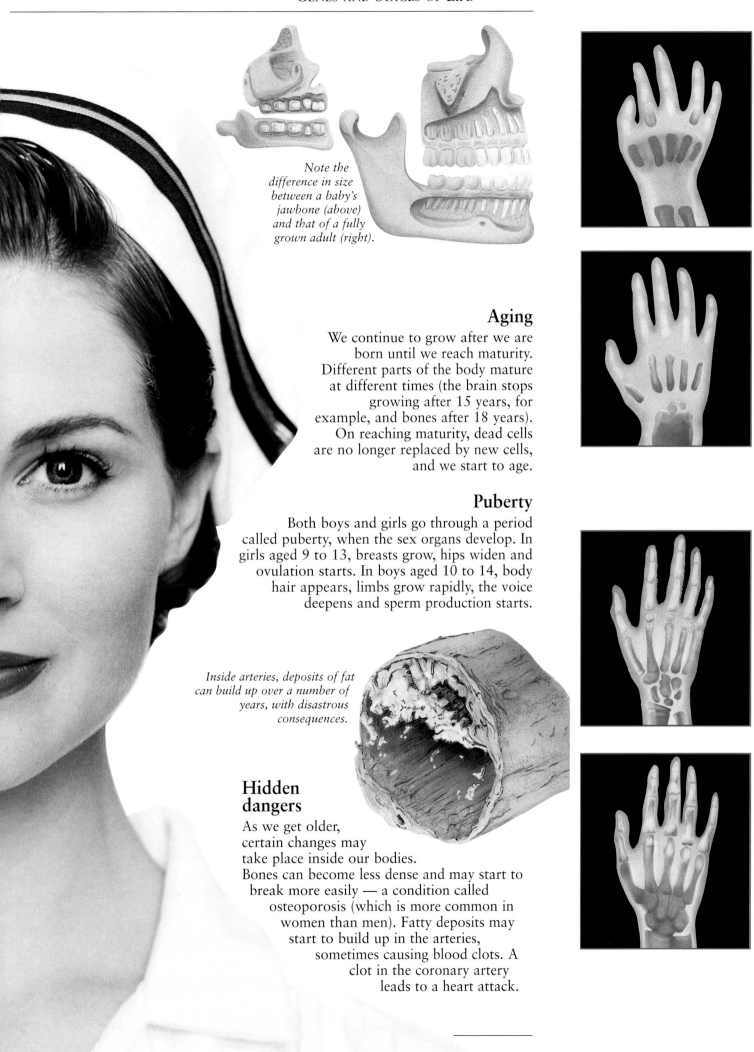

Note the difference in size between a baby's jawbone (above) and that of a fully grown adult (right).

Aging

We continue to grow after we are born until we reach maturity. Different parts of the body mature at different times (the brain stops growing after 15 years, for example, and bones after 18 years). On reaching maturity, dead cells are no longer replaced by new cells, and we start to age.

Puberty

Both boys and girls go through a period called puberty, when the sex organs develop. In girls aged 9 to 13, breasts grow, hips widen and ovulation starts. In boys aged 10 to 14, body hair appears, limbs grow rapidly, the voice deepens and sperm production starts.

Inside arteries, deposits of fat can build up over a number of years, with disastrous consequences.

Hidden dangers

As we get older, certain changes may take place inside our bodies. Bones can become less dense and may start to break more easily — a condition called osteoporosis (which is more common in women than men). Fatty deposits may start to build up in the arteries, sometimes causing blood clots. A clot in the coronary artery leads to a heart attack.

When Things Go Wrong

Below: The lymph system is a vast network that extends throughout the body. Its job is to keep our bodies free from pathogens.

Our bodies are constantly under threat from germs, viruses and harmful bacteria (pathogens) from the outside world. The body has an immune system to tackle these invaders. Our skin is the first line of defense, providing a barrier against the outside world. If pathogens manage to breach this defense, the immune system tries to detect and eliminate them before they can reproduce. If the invader succeeds in reproducing, the immune system immediately goes on the attack.

Lymph system

The lymph system is a vast network that extends throughout the body in a similar way to blood vessels. Running through this system is a clear liquid called lymph, which bathes the body's cells with water and nutrients. Lymph also has the job of detecting and removing pathogens. Lymph is filtered in lymph nodes. Once it has been filtered, it passes into the bloodstream.

White blood cells

It is the job of white blood cells to fight any invading pathogens. All white blood cells are known as leukocytes. They roam independently through the body's tissues, hunting invaders. White blood cells are produced in bone marrow (they cannot divide or reproduce on their own).

How do we know it works?

Our immune system is working all the time. Most of the time we are unaware of it, unless something goes wrong and we get ill. But we can see it working if, for example, we get a splinter in one of our fingers. The immune system responds and eliminates invading bacteria, while the skin repairs itself.

Below: If we get a splinter, the skin may become inflamed, and there may be some pus in the wound, but this is a sign that the immune system is doing its job.

A white blood cell

Other parts of the immune system

Some white blood cells produce antibodies. These are special proteins that respond to a particular virus, bacteria or poison. They work by attaching themselves to an invader so that it cannot move through cell walls. Other proteins that work together with antibodies are produced in the liver. The spleen filters the blood looking for any foreign bodies or red blood cells. All these things work together constantly to prevent us from getting ill.

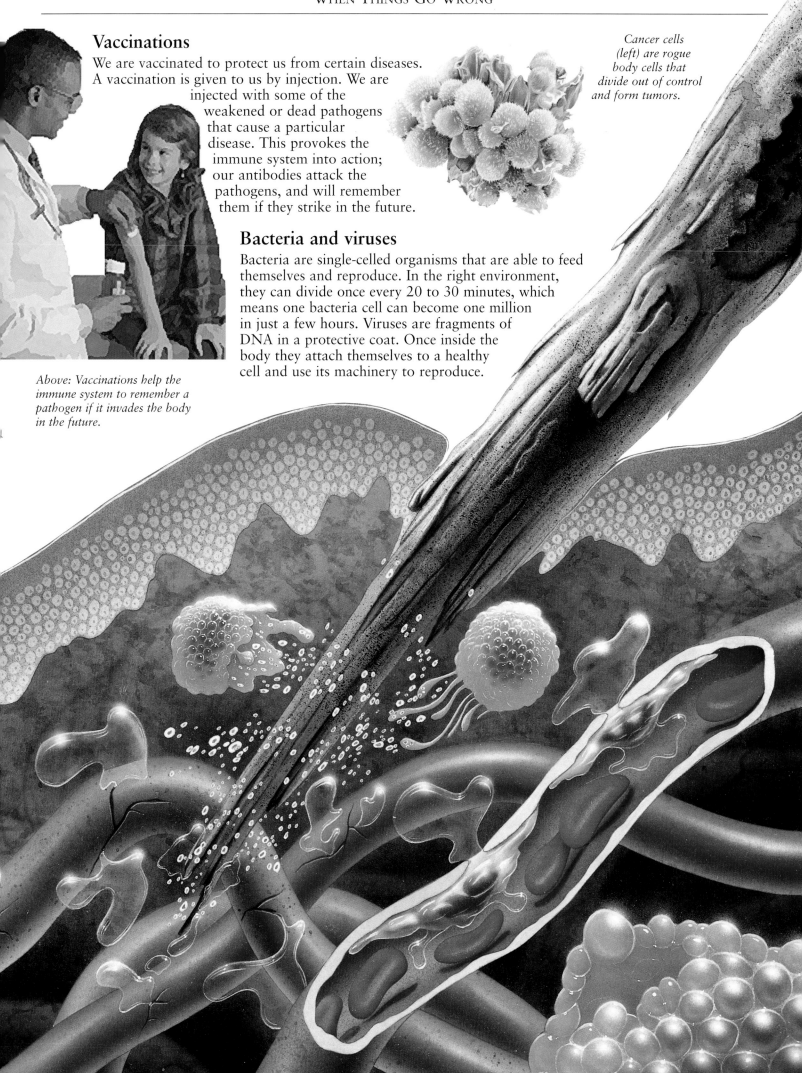

Vaccinations

We are vaccinated to protect us from certain diseases. A vaccination is given to us by injection. We are injected with some of the weakened or dead pathogens that cause a particular disease. This provokes the immune system into action; our antibodies attack the pathogens, and will remember them if they strike in the future.

Cancer cells (left) are rogue body cells that divide out of control and form tumors.

Above: Vaccinations help the immune system to remember a pathogen if it invades the body in the future.

Bacteria and viruses

Bacteria are single-celled organisms that are able to feed themselves and reproduce. In the right environment, they can divide once every 20 to 30 minutes, which means one bacteria cell can become one million in just a few hours. Viruses are fragments of DNA in a protective coat. Once inside the body they attach themselves to a healthy cell and use its machinery to reproduce.

Index